MW01602004

More praise for the book by

"BZ Riger-Hull's warm sprit and creative exercises are a great motivator in making the changes you really want to make in your life."
~ Alison Shaw, photographer, Author of Vineyard Summer

"The *Soul of Success* belongs on the reading list of those who want to listen to their own 'wisdom's voice'. BZ Riger-Hull provides the simple steps, tools, and exercises to take action now."
~ Judy Feld, co-author of SmartMatch Alliances

"Reading and working through the exercises in this book is a great investment in yourself. The *Soul of Success* offers practical tools to get your career and life on track."
~ Doreen Banaszak, CEO, www.DiscoverUniversity.com

"The AM Garbage Papers exercise was amazing! I can't believe how many insightful things I ended up writing down - things that I have never thought before about my life, relationships, etc. I love your book!"
~ Chris Huether, Freelance writer

"A wealth of rich information and straightforward exercises that strategically move you forward bringing clarity and focus to help you determine the best way to build your successful career."
~ Ginger Pozzini, Founder, www.ItalianTravelCoach.com

# *The*

# *Soul*

# *of*

# *Success*

---

## 7 steps to
## monetary and spiritual wealth
## for a rich meaningful life

---

## BZ Riger-Hull

Essence Press, Martha's Vineyard

## Essence Press Martha's Vineyard

For information on ordering books contact:
Essence Press Box 514 West Tisbury MA 02575
Signed copies are available by special request.

Essence Press books are available at special quantity
discounts for bulk purchases for sales promotions,
premiums, fund-raising, and educational needs.

First trade paperback edition published 2002

Library of Congress Catalog Card Number: 002093955

ISBN 0-9721137-9-7

Author's note: The names and details of the client
examples described in this book have been changed to
preserve the confidentiality of the coaching
relationship.

Printed in the United States of America

# Dedication

This book is dedicated to You.

You are wonderful and unique, with valuable gifts to share. It is time to tap your personal power and let the brilliant spirit you are shine.

*"You have to find something that you love enough to be able to take risks, jump over the hurdles and break through the brick walls that are always going to be placed in front of you. If you don't have that kind of feeling for what it is you're doing, you'll stop at the first hurdle."* ~ *George Lucas*

*"Life is meant to be a never-ending education. And when this is fully appreciated. We are no longer survivors but adventurers."* ~ *David McNally*

## Table of Contents

## Acknowledgements

This book would not be possible without the support and friendship of many wonderful people there isn't room to mention each of you by name but that does not diminish my profound gratitude to you. Thank you.

I send a special thought of love and gratitude to these people: my wonderful clients for sharing your triumphs and struggles and for allowing me to walk beside you and witness the depth of your love and courage to recreate your life exactly the way you want it.

Jared, my wonderful husband, for always being there; your quiet support as I have walked along my path to find my heart's desire has been remarkable.

Charlotte, my amazing daughter with your wisdom and fiery spirit, you continue to teach me every day to stoke my passion and reach for my dreams.

Diane, my wonderful coach. Your intuition and love has been my guiding light on an amazing journey to rediscover my brilliance and help me to silence my inner critic so I could write this book.

Andrea, my dear friend and buddy coach. You have such a lovely spirit and zest for fun and celebration- thank you for all of your wise questions as I wrote this book.

Ginger, my dear friend and colleague. Your joyous spirit and loving heart are wonderful gifts generously shared, that pushed me past my doubts and demons as I wrote this book.

Chris, my editor, your gentle hand and insightful suggestions helped me create the best book possible with out the admonishment of the red pen; it's been perfect working with you.

My family for their encouragement and support.

Robin, Jennifer, Diana, Windy, Julie, Debbie, Rob, Barbara, Ann, Kathy, Judy, Margaret, and so many other wonderful people have been in my life and shared so much wisdom with me. I thank all of you.

# Introduction

*"Thought is the blossom, language the bud; action the fruit."*
*~ Ralph Waldo Emerson*

The "soul of success" is our divine nature. It's what our purpose here in the human experience is meant to be. When we tap into the soul of success, we tap into our essence – the unique qualities, gifts, and strengths that we've come to share with the world.

Success is different to everyone. *That's the key.* The old model of success known as "having it all" – the big, fast-paced career, the expensive toys, the family, the accolades – is too vague. There is no soul in this undefined success. Just wanting "the biggest, the best or the next thing" has no meaning unless we are the ones defining what the best is.

We need to clearly define in our own minds what success is. Then we can set out a strategy, develop a plan, and take action to create success on our own terms.

Each one of us must define what is a "rich, meaningful life." *Being excited to get up in the morning. Being excited about what each day will bring. Looking forward to the connections we'll make with people. Striving to make a profound impact in someone's life today.* These are examples of how we will make our lives rich.

Listening to our inner voice, "Wisdom's Voice" and tapping into our essence – *the golden thread that makes us unique and holds our brilliance* – will give our lives meaning. Not being afraid to see our own greatness and share our gifts with the world will produce a monetary and spiritual wealth beyond what we could ever imagine.

This attitude towards success can have a profound impact on everyone we make a connection with in our journey through life.

Too many people live on the "Should Express":

- They go to a certain college, because they think it will please their parents or look good on their resume.

- They stay at a miserable job, because retirement is only a few years away. Since they have stayed this long, they're not going to let the system beat them.

- They put off their passion of starting their own business, because they received a master's degree or have worked their entire life  in one particular field or industry.

What's the worst of all? *"But you don't understand, I don't have a choice."* These people are blinded by the greatest myth of all – they have no choice and staying where they are is the responsible thing to do.

WRONG.

You always have a choice; you just have to consciously face that choice. You need to learn the skills and strategies to live your life totally at choice.

You create what comes into your life. *Where you are right now is the path that you've chosen.* Whether you enjoy it – or not – is a result of the thoughts, feelings, and choices you have made up to this moment.  That's fabulous news.  It means that if you don't like your life now, you can change it.  If you enjoy certain things, you can create more of them.

IT'S YOUR CHOICE.

If you awaken to your inner power – *and consciously make your choices* – you will discover the *soul of success.* And it will be by choice.

I wrote this book to share what I've learned as an entrepreneur and a business women, and what I've helped hundreds of people to discover for themselves. Finding the essence of who you really are – *and what you really want your life and work to do for you* – will give you a rich, meaningful life with monetary and spiritual rewards.

**The soul of success** will guide you to discover your essence, choose your path, and create success on your own terms. You'll remove stress, clutter, frustration, and uncertainty from your life. You'll feel lighter, more balanced and successful.

In this book, I provide seven strategic steps to help take you to the *soul of success.* Step 1 will awaken you to all the possibilities and show you how to commit to yourself. It will also help move you forward through Steps 2-7, which detail how to achieve measurable results from the success that you have defined.

Each step is broken down into three parts with stories, case studies, exercises, and specific how-to's. This easy-to-follow format allows you to not only learn the steps, but also understand how to put each one into practice in your life TODAY!

Life is not a dress rehearsal; it's time to be the star in your life. Read on and apply my seven simple steps to discover your essence. Create a life and career that you are passionate about – and successful in.

Turn the page and let's get started!
BZ Riger-Hull

# Rolling up Your Sleeves

*"Do not follow where the path may lead, go instead where there is no path and leave a trail. Only those who will risk going too far can possibly find out how far they can go."*
~ T.S. Eliot

What I have come to know is that success is comprised of two integral components:

**1)** <mark>DOING OF SUCCESS</mark>
   • Making the right connections
   • Using strategic systems
   • Being motivated by financial gain
   • Striving for external rewards and recognition

**2)** <mark>BEING OF SUCCESS</mark>
   • Doing what you love
   • Living in integrity
   • Being motivated by making a contribution
   • Being effortlessly propelled by your passion

*It's not either / or... it is imperative to have both.*

*Just doing* comes at a very high price:
- Stress
- Divorce
- Burnout
- Emptiness (Is this all there is?!)
- Overwhelm
- A sense something is missing

*Just being* is a little healthier but comes at a high price, too:
- Lack of systems
- Too many distractions
- Struggle with accepting financial rewards
- Emptiness (There must be a better way!)
- Overwhelm
- A sense something is missing

You step into the *soul of success* when you can dance with these two components and let them course effortlessly through your life. These two components act as a seesaw in the flow of your life.

Consciously riding this seesaw is not only fun. It will dramatically improve the quality of your life, removing struggle, stress, and longing.

By mastering the art of riding, you can use this seesaw to help create a rich, meaningful life. You will have success beyond your wildest dreams.

But more importantly, you will have the courage to be brilliant, the courage to step into your own greatness and to share your unique gifts with others. Mastering the art of riding provides the opportunity to contribute *"your"* missing piece that was God's gift to you and your gift in the journey of the human experience.

My contribution and passion is helping people find success in its *absolute* form- by helping them remember the essence of who they really are. And sharing with them the tools and strategies to master the art of riding the seesaw to the *soul of success*.

*"The game of life is a game of boomerangs. Our thoughts, deeds and words return to us sooner or later with astounding accuracy."* ~ *Florence Scovel Shinn*

I have balanced precariously in the air on each side of what I like to call the "seesaw of success." This term represents the constant teetering that each one of us experiences between the BEING OF SUCCESS and the DOING OF SUCCESS.

The DOING OF SUCCESS overshadowed my childhood – the protestant work ethic, long hours, and constant struggle and stress for external rewards and recognition. Oh sure, our family had many of the things associated with being "successful" – the vacation home on Martha's Vineyard, the private schools, lots of gifts after the latest television assignment, etc.

But perched at that altitude on the seesaw of success, I experienced the nosebleeds caused by the DOING OF SUCCESS – the overwhelm and constant verbal lashings of being better, doing more, not being good enough, and being lazy. There was divorce, emptiness, and snuffing out of the creative spirit. However, my costs paled in comparison to the high price my parents suffered from the DOING OF SUCCESS. Stress, judgment, sacrifice, struggle, loneliness...both their lives were ended by cancer.

After growing up spending most of my time learning, experiencing, and trying out the DOING OF SUCCESS side of the seesaw and mixing that up with the rebellious tendencies of a teenager, I set out on my own life journey determined to do it differently!

I spent the next phase of my life – you've probably guessed it – on the BEING OF SUCCESS side of the seesaw. I followed my passion for horses into a career as an eventing coach I combined my love for horses and entrepreneurial spirit to create the first of many "successful" entrepreneurial adventures with a company I started called "Pony Express Horse Trailering".

This side of the seesaw was pretty high, too. Sometimes, it came crashing down. Sometimes as I rode, I would get yanked in a turbulent gust of wind back to the other side of the seesaw.

The bruises on this side of the seesaw were minor lessons caused by scuffs on the road of life. Or they were self-inflicted lashings from the inner critic learned from the excellent modeling by my parents.

Looking back on it, I did pretty well considering I was not consciously riding the seesaw of success yet.

Falling in love and having a daughter were a wonderful part of the BEING OF SUCCESS; nevertheless, there were plenty of downsides, too. The most important thing I gained was the awareness of the seesaw of success. I had a shift in my perspective and could clearly see that there were two integral parts to success.

It was not until my mother died of cancer when I was 29 years of age that I consciously began to ride the seesaw of success. It was a completely new experience. By being aware and consciously riding, I discovered that the seesaw really was fun. This awareness dramatically improved the quality of my life.

As part of my riding lessons, I cleared away cracks in my foundation and Limiting Beliefs that no longer served me. I worked really hard at combining my DOING OF SUCCESS with my BEING OF SUCCESS. Things started to flow. I created a business – one that I was passionate about – which was based on both sides of the seesaw of success. It gave me time to spend with my young daughter and family. In addition, this business was customer-centered, giving lots of tangible and intangible value to my clients.

For a while, everything worked really well. However, the "doing" (and lots of it!) crept in when I was not looking. It clouded my conscious laser focus of riding the seesaw.

You know the familiar saying: "Old habits die hard." Once again, I woke up to an awareness of consciously riding the seesaw of success. I looked at what was missing, what was calling me, and where I wanted to go. "IT" was coaching and sharing my gifts, passions, and lessons learned with people like you.

I have stayed conscious and kept my laser focus of awareness on the seesaw. And wow, it's great fun to ride the seesaw of success this way!

One of my life goals is to MASTER riding the seesaw of success. I have gained great proficiency over the last several years. My work as a coach has helped me come to be on familiar terms with the *soul of success*. Even though I still come crashing down now and then, I am well on my way to mastering the art of riding the seesaw and fully achieving the *soul of success*.

> *"The world can only be grasped by action, not by contemplation... The hand is the cutting edge of the mind."*
> ~ *Jacob Bronowski*

I wrote this book to share the seven strategic steps of the Essence Strategy©, so you can become aware of the two integral components of success.

Helping you to consciously see the seesaw and ultimately master riding it to attain the *soul of success* was my intention for writing the book.

### *You can experience success in a new dimension*

All of you who are reading this book are successful to a certain degree. My intention is to move you to a new level of success. This level is one that YOU create – one that is structured, carried out, and enjoyed on *your own terms!*

There is a lot of valuable material out there for readers on the topic of success. However, my intention is to give you a book that stands apart by moving out of the theoretical to the practical. This book gives you the tools to actually create your own success.

When you write a book, one of the questions you are supposed to answer is "what makes what you have to say different and unique?" As I sat to ponder this question, my inner critic – true to form – jumped right in. "Not much!" were the first words that I heard. I thanked my inner critic for the input. Then I really pondered what I thought about the question and what my answer was.

Sometimes I find myself challenging some of the things I hear and read. Sometimes, I get belligerent around certain topics or notions. This feeling is not necessarily towards the writer or the concept. I think it's more to challenge what I think about it and how the concepts appear or affect my life view.

This happened when I was thinking about the question of "what do you have to say that is unique?" I decided that the book was unique for three reasons:

- First, I was writing it. Therefore, my life experiences and my voice made it unique.

- Second, I was combining the theme of success and the theme spirituality, which in my life has created a confluence to share the view of success in its *absolute* form.

- Third, and most importantly, my intention was to write a book that would be unique to each person whom worked through the exercises and read the steps and case studies. The book would be unique because you would bring something special to the "IT."

### What song do you have to sing and how can this book help you do it?

The perfect gift would be for you to share this work within your area of expertise. Whether it be a teacher...speaker...author...parent...CEO...manager...director of a non-profit organization...entrepreneur...

How can you continually create a unique tool to help you create the life you really want? Simply tailor the information and exercises so they work for you.

*"Desire, like the atom, is explosive with creative force."*
*~ Paul Vernon Buser*

My intention with this book is to encourage and support you to be courageous and create your life by choice. You are perfect where you are right now and having an awareness of that will allow you to consciously look at what is really important to you. I want to get you to think- to ponder what you want more of in your life and what you are ready to let go of .

Here is your invitation to move into the book – your invitation to start a new journey. This book is not at all about fixing. It's about taking small steps. Making choices. Taking action.

### Be yourself and shine brightly!

# STEP 1

## Coming to Consciousness

*"I know of no more encouraging fact than the unquestionable ability of man to elevate his life by conscious endeavor."*
                                        ~ *Henry David Thoreau*

What is "coming to consciousness"? It's an awakening to what you are passionate about in your life. You realize that with your thoughts and feelings, you create the desire and vision. Then you create what happens in your life.

You may be thinking: "Wait a minute. I'm already conscious. I wake up every morning...wash the sleep out of my body...and get on with my day."

Yes, you awaken every day from a state of sleep. Get dressed. And start your routine. What I'm talking about is living consciously. *You really wake up to everything around you.* Every sight. Every sound. Every thought. Every decision that you make.

Breathing is an involuntary system. It keeps air going in and out of the body; you don't have to think about it. For most people, 92% of breathing is shallow and short – just enough to keep the air coming in. However, this type of breathing doesn't support a rich, meaningful exchange of oxygen in the body.

Deep, oxygenated breathing expands your lung capacity. It sends oxygen-rich blood to your muscles, giving them power to support any activity you choose to do. Conscious breathing takes a deep, full breath down to your abdomen...fills up your lungs...and sends oxygen coursing out to the tiniest capillaries. This type of breathing supplies your whole body with exactly what it needs.

Have you let your life become involuntary? Is it a shallow exploration of your talents and gifts – just enough to keep things coming in, but not enough to support a rich, meaningful life?

## Case Study: Deep in the Numbness of Daily Life

My friend Kara's life had become involuntary. She was a project manager at a design firm. Twelve years ago, Kara started working part-time at the firm to earn extra income for a summer trip to Europe. Her vision was to spend three months traveling by train, stopping in towns that caught her eye, and exploring what she wanted to spend her life doing.

Doubts about the trip, criticism from her family, and the hectic pace of her part-time job (which was evolving into more of a full-time position every week) slowly eroded away Kara's confidence. She began to question the value of taking three months to really think about what she wanted from her life and career. You can probably guess what happened to the Europe trip.

Kara felt a drone from all the "should's" her family and co-workers bombarded her with each week – and from thinking that the job wasn't what she really wanted to be doing. However, the job did provide good health insurance. And she enjoyed some of the accounts that she managed.

Kara was deep in the numbness of daily life, when she received a phone call. Her father had suffered a heart attack. He was admitted to the hospital. Four weeks later, he died of complications

Fourteen months passed by. Kara found herself more stressed, irritable, and very dissatisfied. She thought, "It's time to wake up and get conscious." Just this recognition of being unconscious in her life helped Kara open up to new possibilities. A large client of the firm needed someone to handle a new project on location – in Italy! Kara was given the account.

After completing the project, Kara used eight weeks of back vacation time to travel in Italy. While she was in Europe, Kara planned to figure out what her next step in life would be.

## *Case Study: A Desire to Do Something New*

My friend Toni had been working as a teacher for 16 years. She loved the job and the connections she made with the kids. However, the politics in the school were really wearing on her. She was torn between wanting to leave her teaching job – and do something new that really inspired her – or staying two more years to collect her retirement health benefits. Toni decided to take a sabbatical to recharge and get back her love for teaching.

I ran into Toni at the dance studio. We chatted about what she had been up to. I noticed that Toni had lost weight and looked younger. Her eyes seemed to sparkle. I said, "You look great! Taking a break from the school really seems to agree with you."

She responded, "I'm still trying to decide between not returning to teaching...or staying two more years to collect the health benefit."

I replied, "If being out of the teaching environment on sabbatical has made such a difference already...is it really worth *the risk of the health consequences* of returning for two more years – just to get the health benefit?"

I ran into Toni again six weeks later. She had made the decision to leave the school system. Toni had not only lost 20 pounds, but she also had been offered two jobs. Getting conscious was really beginning to pay off for her.

#### ---- Exercise ----
#### <u>How Conscious Are You?</u>

Rate your level of consciousness for each of the following activities (1 = barely aware and just going through the motions; 10 = very conscious and alert to your thoughts, feelings, and actions):

\_\_\_\_ On my way to work, I smile at the people I see along the way.

\_\_\_\_ When I eat, I enjoy my food and can easily describe what it tastes like.

\_\_\_\_ When someone compliments me about my work, I honestly accept and hear it.

\_\_\_\_ When I am listening to people, I am totally focused and not thinking about what I'm going to say when they're done talking.

\_\_\_\_ I pay attention to my gut-intuition.

\_\_\_\_ At work, I notice if people in my department are upset.

\_\_\_\_ I have no trouble remembering details of specific tasks I did at the beginning of the week.

\_\_\_\_ I wake up in the morning refreshed and ready to enjoy the day.

--------

### Recognizing two traps that limit your success

Coming to consciousness must be a choice. It's an active decision that you make to awaken. However, there are two traps that limit many of us from choosing to become conscious.

One trap that we fall into is NEGATIVE THOUGHTS. We don't acknowledge our thoughts and ability to take action. As a result, we create a state of unconsciousness filled with negativity.

A second trap is NOT LIVING OUR OWN LIVES. We have dreams and desires. But instead of consciously choosing our plan and following our dreams, we let other people pull and shape our thoughts. We conform to what they think is good for us – or what makes THEM feel more comfortable.

Have you ever noticed that many people are threatened when you change, grow, and make positive shifts in your life? These positive changes make them feel uncomfortable, because things aren't working in THEIR lives. They feel stuck in a particular situation.

Or perhaps they want something more out of life, but don't have the courage or commitment to bring their desires into sharper focus.

It's time to discover where you are right now – how conscious you are, and what you like and don't like about your life.

### Ask Yourself: How Satisfying is My Life & Work?

What are the positive and negative sides of where you are right now? By looking at both your likes and dislikes, you'll get a better perspective. The essence of what you really want will become clear.

General statements like "I hate my job" or "I want to make more money" only serve as complaints with no action or clarity. They do not reveal the essence of your core dissatisfaction. "I want to lose weight" or "I wish I could be my own boss" are just daydreaming and wishful thinking. Again, you're not clarifying or developing a plan of action.

Writing down the specifics of where you are – *describing your feelings, and identifying the satisfaction and dissatisfaction in specific areas of your life and work* – will enable you to discover the essence of your strengths. You'll find out what's holding you back.

### Case Study: Unhappy But Unsure of New Direction

Sarah was unhappy with her position. She wanted a change, but she wasn't sure of the best direction for her. After completing the Life and Work Satisfaction Assessments, Sarah discovered the essence of her dissatisfactions and her strengths. She was able to clearly see that she wanted to stay in the same company, but move to the marketing division. Sarah could then apply her strategic and people skills, which would give her more satisfaction.

It's now time to begin to discover your *"soul of success."* Start a journal, notebook or computer file. Use it to record your answers to the following two satisfaction assessments. Be very specific with your answers. Get to the essence of what you like and don't like, rather than making vague, generalized statements. Write down your first reactions; be honest with yourself.

#### ---- Exercise ----

### Life Satisfaction Assesment

In your journal, notebook or computer file, answer each of the following statements by writing what first comes to your mind. Don't edit your responses!

- What I DON'T like about my LIVING SPACE right now *(things to change)*

- What I DO like about my LIVING SPACE right now *(things to preserve)*

- What I DON'T like about how I spend my FREE TIME each day *(things to change)*

- What I DO like about how I spend my FREE TIME each day *(things to preserve)*

- What I DON'T like about my FRIENDSHIPS right now *(things to change)*

- What I DO like about my FRIENDSHIPS right now *(things to preserve)*

- What I DON'T like about how I spend my time on the WEEKENDS *(things to change)*

- What I DO like about how I spend my time on the WEEKENDS *(things to preserve)*

--------

---- **Exercise** ----

## Work Satisfaction Assesment

In your journal, notebook or computer file, answer each of the following statements by writing what first comes to your mind. Don't edit your responses!

- What I DON'T like about MY RESPONSIBILITIES at the office right now *(things to change)*

- What I DO like about MY RESPONSIBILITIES at the office right now *(things to preserve)*

- What I DON'T like about HOW I SPEND MY TIME each day *(things to change)*

- What I DO like about HOW I SPEND MY TIME each day *(things to preserve)*

- What I DON'T like about MY RELATIONSHIPS AT WORK right now *(things to change)*

- What I DO like about MY RELATIONSHIPS AT WORK right now *(things to preserve)*

- What I DON'T like about MY STYLE IN WORKING WITH PEOPLE right now *(things to change)*

- What I DO like about MY STYLE IN WORKING WITH PEOPLE right now *(things to preserve)*

--------

## PART 1

### Figure out the pebble in your shoe

*"By asking for the impossible, we obtain the best possible. "*
> ~ *Italian saying*

You'll need a new perspective for viewing your life and your career. The following exercise is a new method for going through your day and your week. It's a new sense of being alive – being responsible, being at choice, and being the architect in your life.

Tomorrow, you'll be totally conscious about everything you do, see, say, feel, smell, taste, and who you are being. Use your notebook, journal or computer file to capture notes, thoughts, and insights.

**---- Exercise ----**

### A Totally Conscious Day

Notice everything! Write down your observations using 1-2 words or several sentences. There is no wrong or right way to do it.

- As soon as you wake up, notice the first thoughts that enter your mind. Write them down. Go into the bathroom. Look into the mirror. Look into your eyes. *Really look!* Smile. Spend a minute looking into your eyes. Smile goodbye. Write down feelings or thoughts you experienced.

- As you get ready for work, notice everything – the rhythm of brushing your teeth, brushing your hair, the motion your arm makes as you stroke on your makeup, etc. Write down any thoughts or describe any pictures that come to mind.

- On your way to work, notice your surroundings. What are the buildings like? What does your route to work smell like? Can you smell the restaurants, factories, etc? Do you smell trees in bloom? As you get closer to work, what sensations do you notice in your body? Write down every observation.

- When the day is over, spend a few quiet minutes in bed reading your notes. Do you remember things you didn't capture before? Write them down in <u>a different color pen</u> than your notes from earlier in the day. Finally, spend five minutes writing your impressions of what you captured and what you experienced being totally conscious.

--------

This exercise provides a lot of perspective and insight, but you have to actually DO it – not just read the directions and say, "That sounds like a great idea. I'll try it later."

It's really important to "get clear." This first step is critical to your success. If you make the decision to become conscious – *to become completely aware of what is really going on* – you become aware of what it is that you really want.

We often become excited after participating in a workshop, attending a seminar or reading a book. We think, "Oh, this is it. This is the thing that's going to change my life." However, we don't make the decision to start, to take action. Or we may think that by simply reading a book, it will somehow magically change our lives: "The information is going to float over me... and my life is going to be different."

When the pebble in our shoe bugs us enough, we pick up a book or attend a seminar. *We briefly take off our shoe.* We enjoy the comfort of the idea of not traveling with the pebble in our shoe anymore.

When the seminar or book is finished, we put our shoe back on over the pebble. Then we start our journey again. We feel a little lighter and more enthusiastic, because of encountering new material. So the pebble is barely noticeable. However, we never made a decision – *a conscious choice* – to remove the pebble or get shoes that keep the pebble from falling back in again.

We never really get started.

### Case Study:  The Low Grade, Quiet Nag Pebble

Eleanor spent three years walking around with a pebble in her shoe. A happy, lifelong learner, she enjoyed going to workshops and reading self-help and business life books. Eleanor would tell her friends about the books and workshop experiences. She could really see the value of the messages being presented. However, she would always put back on her shoe and continue walking with the pebble.

Eleanor's pebble was small but very hard – what I call the "low grade, quiet nag pebble." *It's the worst kind of pebble to have in your shoe.* It's not large or painful enough to drive you crazy. You just have to stop and remove it often – whenever it can't be ignored any longer.

Some days, this pebble rolls under the ball of your foot and really bugs you. Other days, it rolls to the little extra space in the toe of your shoe. You can sense that the pebble is still there, but there's no obvious sign of it.

Eleanor and I had been working together for a few weeks. She wanted to make a change in her life, but she wasn't sure what it was. Eleanor's job was interesting. Her benefits were pretty good. Her salary provided a comfortable living. However, she didn't really feel excited or fulfilled by anything.

I noticed that Eleanor mentioned different books and workshops that she had attended. She recommended that friends and colleagues try the exercises. However, she never discussed how the exercises had worked for her. I asked Eleanor, "When you come to an exercise, do you answer the questions? Or do you think 'those are good questions' ... and then look to see what you MAY have scored – IF you had actually stopped and done the exercise?"

With a sheepish giggle, Eleanor said that she never really did any of the exercises. When things weren't going smoothly – *and that pebble in her shoe rolled to a painful spot* – she found herself thinking about a particular exercise. She said, "I guess that's one of the reasons I hired you."

Within a month of completing exercises to help address the pebble in her shoe, Eleanor decided it was time to make some changes. Although still not sure of the direction she wanted to take, Eleanor was finally very clear about removing the pebble and taking action.

Whether you know what you want to do – or no longer want that quiet, nag pebble in your shoe – the realization that you need to make a change and take action is a great place to be. When you make the decision to move forward, it's truly a momentous occasion.

Today, you are finally awake.

### ---- Exercise ----

### Today is the Day

On a blank page in your journal, notebook or computer file. Write down today's date then write down your decision to move forward and consciously choose what you bring into your life.

Describe a specific direction and intention you want to make happen. If you have no specific direction yet, write a clear intention of moving forward and exploring new opportunities.

--------

No more shallow breathing. No more involuntary living. You've chosen to come to consciousness. *Today is the day that you are going to wake up.* You're going to become conscious to the limitless possibilities in your life. They're just ready for you to create. Whatever has gone before – whatever has gotten in your way in the past – no longer matters. You're going to change things. You're going to move forward.

The following scale is a deceptively simple tool that I use with my clients. It helps gauge how ready they are to make the decision to move forward. How ready are you?

---- **Exercise** ----
## Passion and Pain Scale

**Pain**
Rate yourself from 1-10 on the level of pain (i.e. emotional, financial, overwhelm, dissatisfaction, actual pain from physical work) you are currently experiencing in your life. Mark the number on the scale below:

< 1 _____5_____10>


**Passion**
Rate yourself from 1-10 on the level of passion (i.e. emotional, financial, challenge, fulfillment, actual passion envisioning your own business) you feel about the changes you want to bring into your life. Mark the number on the scale below:

< 1 _____5_____10>

Why is this exercise helpful? PAIN is a great tool for pushing you forward, breaking inertia, and creating momentum. PASSION is a great tool for pulling you forward, sustaining motivation, and building on momentum.

Don't worry whether you scored in the 8-10 range or the 4-5 range on either scale. These scores are both excellent results, which you can use to move forward – to strengthen your decision and look at your desire and vision.

--------

# PART 2

## Figure out the essence of what you want

*"We set our sights on a destination beyond the distant horizon, and then 'we make the road by walking.'"*
~ *Myles Horton & Paulo Freire*

By first clearing out of your mind what you don't like, you can clear out confusion and resistance to moving forward.

You'll figure out the answers to many important questions like, what is important to you? What is the essence of what you want from your life and your relationships? What is the essence of what you want your work, career and business to do for you? What do you want to contribute? What gifts do you have to share? What is the vehicle you want to use to bring these gifts to the world?

Look back at the "Life and Work Satisfaction Assessments" that you did earlier in Step 1. As you complete the following exercise, focus on the dislikes you included in those assessments – the things that you want to change or replace in your life and work.

#### ---- Exercise ----

### Mining your Dislikes

In your journal, notebook or computer file, build a list about the specifics of what you don't like in your life and work. Use headings to focus your thoughts. FRIENDSHIPS, LIVING SPACE, BOSS, EMPLOYEES, CO-WORKERS, RESPONSIBILITIES, STYLE OF COMMUNICATING
WITH OTHERS, ETC.

Remember, you need to be very specific about what you don't like. Being specific gives you a powerful tool to turn the dislikes from a position of complaining reaction to EMPOWERED ACTION – a request you can make of yourself, someone else or the universe. It sets things on a different path. It gives you a new footing.

Don't make general statements like, "My boss drives me nuts." *Get to the essence of what you don't like.* For example, "My boss speaks very loudly and fast. It always rattles me, even when I am confident about the project that I am working on. It makes me feel small and powerless."

Be thorough. Explore all of the things you don't like. Be sure to look at the little things, which can build the pebbles in your shoe.

--------

## Case Study: Getting Specific for Greater Results

Roger found this part of Step 1 to be invaluable for realizing how to improve his management style.

Initially, his list of dislikes was very unspecific. It read more like a long, whining complaint than a discovery of the essence of what he didn't like. This was particularly apparent when Roger wrote about people that he managed in the IT division.

He created a second list. This time, he was very specific. Roger included his feelings and reactions in situations he didn't like – or when dealing with an employee whose behavior or work style he didn't like.

After coaching Roger through this exercise, I requested that he ask some of his employees to try it. Roger knew that – in order for this request to be successful – he would have to establish a foundation of trust. His employees needed to really believe they could honestly share their dislikes about work. He accepted my request as a fun challenge.

Roger wanted to start with a small group, before bringing the idea to his whole department. He decided to coach four members of his staff on the process of mining their dislikes. He chose two employees that he easily managed and two employees that were more difficult. Working with each one individually, Roger asked the employees to build a clear, specific, and honest list of what they didn't like about their work.

He was amazed by the things on their lists – especially from the two employees he had been having challenges with. He found the lists to be very thoughtful and specific. He was able to coach the employees into finding the essence of what they didn't like. Roger turned the dislikes that they shared – *how they wanted to be managed; changes that would make them productive and more fulfilled in their work* – into action.

The results were very powerful. Roger's division improved their team effectiveness and productivity. Even the VP of his division noticed how Roger's staff seemed more happy and enthusiastic about work. Sick days decreased 31%, and they finished two large projects a month ahead of schedule.

### Case Study:  Getting to the Essence of Dislikes

At first, Robyn had trouble with this exercise. Although she wasn't thrilled with her life, Robyn had difficulty identifying the specifics – really getting at the essence of what she didn't like about things. So we broke it down into small steps.

Robyn found her roommate, Jane, was too unpredictable. Robyn loved being with Jane. They were very close friends. But Jane was always coming up with new ideas for redecorating their room or changing her mind at the last minute about their plans for going out. Robyn couldn't put her finger on what really bothered her about Jane. She just felt flustered and unsettled by all her roommate's new ideas. Robyn wasn't willing to consider moving. She just felt uncomfortable.

As we looked a little deeper, Robyn discovered her mother had habits similar to Jane's. However, her mother was very unpredictable and unreliable. Robyn remembered that when she was seven years old, her mother changed plans at the last minute and forgot to pick her up at dance. She waited two hours before her mother showed up. Robyn was embarrassed and angry. As the years went by, her mother become more unreliable –

always changing plans, running late, forgetting to pick Robyn up.

Robyn reacted by getting very organized and structured. She planned everything out to the last detail, in order to avoid the feelings of fear, embarrassment, and anger that she felt growing up.

By completing the "Mining Your Dislikes" exercise, Robyn discovered her admiration for her roommate's freedom, and her ability to be spontaneous - and live in the moment. *Robyn also discovered that she disliked her own inability to be spontaneous.* Once she got to the essence of what she didn't like, Robyn could reframe these dislikes – and take action to create more of what she wanted in her life.

Stop settling. Stop putting up with those pebbles in your shoe. *Notice them. List them. Get them all out in the open.* Then take action and turn those pebbles into points of possibility.

### ---- Exercise ----

### Sift and Find Your Passion

In your journal, notebook or computer file, build a list about the specifics of what you really like in your life and work. Use headings to focus your thoughts. RELATIONSHIPS, HOME, BUSINESS, COLLEAGUES, FINANCES, CHALLENGES, STYLE OF WORKING WITH OTHERS, etc.

Don't make general statements like, "I like my work." *Get to the essence of what you really like.* For example, "My work with people gives me a sense of meaning. I feel like I'm making a real contribution helping people. It comes so naturally to me, it gives me a lot of joy."

Be thorough. Explore all of the things you really like. Be sure to look at the little things. These things give you small, brilliant flashes of joy that combine to make a great day, week, year, and life.

--------

## Case Study: A New Outlook on Life

Cecilia was very energized by the "Sift and Find Your Passion" exercise. She had grown up with parents and an older brother who had modeled being victims. Everything was always a struggle. You could never count on things staying the way you wanted them, so it was important to always be prepared for the worst.

After the exercise, Cecilia realized there were many little things that she really enjoyed doing in life. She also discovered she was an optimist. At least once while creating her list, Cecilia removed the "should" of having to be prepared for the worst.

Working on the list changed her whole outlook at work, too. Cecilia was the managing sales director for her company's Southwest division. After four years of working in this position, it didn't seem like she was going to move any further. With her new perspective, Cecilia found herself being more supportive of her sales staff. She started to look for the positives rather than the downside when faced with challenges.

Within one year, Cecilia was promoted to VP and her sales region was expanded to cover the South and Mid Atlantic regions.

## Case Study: A Fresh Perspective about Work

Brian's list was very short. He really couldn't find anything in his life that he really liked. It mirrored his dislike list, which was also very short. I had spent the last four months coaching together with Brian, working on expanding his business. He owned a lawn and garden shop, which offered engine repair services, as well as selling plants and some gift items in the florist section.

Brian liked the business, but was dissatisfied with his profit. Although he was eager to make changes and grow the business, Brian was having a hard time making any progress.

We took another look at his " Passion and Pain Scale." Brian had given himself a "5" rating on both scales. Despite his dissatisfaction and desire to do things differently, Brian wasn't feeling enough PAIN to push him forward – or enough PASSION to pull him forward and sustain any momentum.

Brian said he really didn't like where his business was. He didn't like how he felt when he was at work or home. He just felt numb to all the work and lack of time in his life. He used up so much energy just trying to get past his feeling of frustration and physical fatigue, it was difficult to sustain any enthusiasm for moving forward in the direction he really wanted.

We looked at the essence of what he really wanted his business to do for him – what revenue he wanted it to generate, what kinds of things he enjoyed selling, what types of services he really wanted to provide, what things he liked most about his favorite customers. Then we looked at the essence of what he wanted in his life – what was really important to him, and what was his measure of success.

Once he focused on the ESSENCE of who he was – and what he wanted his life and work to do for him – Brian was able to come up with a bigger vision of what was possible. Once he focused on his VISION, Brian was able to remove certain services and products from his business. Then he enhanced the areas that he enjoyed. These changes brought greater profit in money and fulfillment. After nine months, Brian was well on his way to turning the business and his life around. He was consciously choosing what he wanted – and he enjoyed making it happen.

He expanded the florist section by hiring Joan, who had a great eye for arrangements and a talent for business. She incorporated a design area. She collaborated with local photographers and wedding consultants to run bridal shows and other seminars to help brides plan their weddings.

Brian also leased out the repair facility to an entrepreneur who really loved fixing things. This change freed up Brian. Instead of spending time doing something he wasn't passionate about, Brian could now provide a valuable service to his customers – *a new service that incorporated his bigger vision into the nursery side of the business.*

Because it incorporated his vision, this service was the best part of Brian's business redesign. Brian developed a plant-breeding program. He collaborated with local high schools and community colleges to offer horticulture courses, which included a work training program to provide students with the opportunity to get experience and learn a trade.

These changes made a big difference in Brian's profit. He accumulated not only wealth, but also a feeling of passion in his life.

The work you have done so far has helped you get conscious – to look at where you are right now. You've made the decision to move forward and make changes, clearing out what you don't like and discovering the essence of what you really do like.

Now you'll create a bigger vision for yourself and your life. You must realize that you hold the power to see, create, and live the bigger vision. This vision comes from YOU – not your boss, your business, your family or your circumstances. *You have the power and the choice to create what you want.*

#### ---- Exercise ----

### Getting Ready for a Bigger Vision

Write down answers to the following questions in your journal, notebook or computer file:

- How would you rate the quality of your life today (including both your business and personal life)?
- What does success mean to you? List three things that you use to define success on your own terms.

- If you chose not hold back in your life, what would you be doing?

--------

Following is a wonderful teaching story that I've seen in many publications and Internet sites. Although the author's name is unknown, I want to share it with you now. Use these simple, wise words for reflection and as a platform to launch your bigger vision.

### *The Mountain Story*

*A son and his father were walking in the mountains. Suddenly, his son falls, hurts himself and screams: "AAAhhhhhhhhhhh!!!"*

*To his surprise, he hears the voice repeating, somewhere in the mountain: "AAAhhhhhhhhhhhh!!!"*

*Curious, he yells: "Who are you?"*
*He receives the answer: "Who are you?"*
*And then he screams to the mountain: "I admire you!"*
*The voice answers: "I admire you!"*
*Angered at the response, he screams: "Coward!"*
*He receives the answer: "Coward!"*

*He looks to his father and asks: "What's going on?"*
*The father smiles and says: "My son, pay attention."*
*Again the man screams: "You are a champion!"*
*The voice answers: "You are a champion!"*
*The boy is surprised, but does not understand.*

*Then the father explains:*
*"People call this ECHO, but really this is LIFE.*
*It gives you back everything you say or do.*

*Our life is simply a reflection of our actions.*
*If you want more love in the world, create more love in your heart.*
*If you want more competence in your team, improve your competence. This relationship applies to everything, in all aspects of life; Life will give you back everything you have given to it."*

*YOUR LIFE IS NOT A COINCIDENCE.*
*IT'S A REFLECTION OF YOU!"* ~ *Anonymous*

Why was Brian so successful in turning his lawn and garden shop around? He tapped into a bigger vision of what he wanted his business to do for him. Brian realized that by staying *stuck down* in the business – instead of putting his efforts into *working* on the business – he wasn't supporting his needs or desires. He got conscious about what he really wanted, and made a decision to change things.

By looking to the essence of what really excited and gave him satisfaction about his work, Brian created a bigger vision that expanded his business, his wealth, and his fulfillment. It also greatly reduced the number of hours he worked.

As you complete the following exercise, thoughtfully review the previous notes from your journal, notebook or computer file. It will help generate a vision that will inspire, energize and challenge you to bring the essence of who you truly are to all areas of your life and work.

#### ---- Exercise ----
#### Building a Bigger Vision

Answer the following questions in your journal, notebook or computer file.

- Think of someone you admire and make a list of all of the qualities that you think makes him or her successful.
- Think of a business that you highly regard and make a list of all the contributions you think it makes to the world.
- If money wasn't a concern, what kind of business would you create or work in?
- What would you like to be remembered for?
- What really gives you a feeling of satisfaction?
- What would you like to do that will have a profound impact in people's lives?
- If you didn't make any changes in your life, what will you be doing in 5 years? What will you be doing in 10 years?

* If you get conscious about creating your life, what will be doing in 5 years?  How about 10 years?

--------

## *PART 3*

### *Give your word; make a commitment to you*

*"No great thing is created suddenly, any more than a bunch of grapes or a fig. If you tell me that you desire a fig, I answer you that there must be time. Let it first blossom, then bear fruit, then ripen."*
~ *Epictetus*

The third part of Step 1 is making a commitment to you – committing that you are priceless and worthy of the investment in time, energy, thought, emotion, and courage that it will take to get off autopilot and consciously live your life.

No more whining sessions or complaining about your life.  No more blaming other people and circumstances for limiting your success. No more settling for someone else's measure of success, which leaves you without the *soul of success* – and the rich life provided by it.

It's time to make a commitment to yourself.  It's time to put aside the Limiting Beliefs.  Put aside the what-ifs.  Put aside, "Oh, but you don't understand, I don't have a choice."

### *Case Study:  Making the Commitment*

Gina struggled with this part of Step 1.  She was a producer at one of the top television networks. However, Gina wasn't happy.  She was burnt out.  The "glamorous life" of working with celebrities and pulling down a hefty salary just wasn't satisfying her.

Her career had been an exhilarating ride with accolades, awards, connections with movers and shakers, and dates with handsome men.  Her friends would always say, "I wish I was you!" Gina seemed so successful; they envied her lifestyle – big house, sports car, gorgeous guys. Her family was proud that she "made it big" and "had it all."

Gina tried to make changes in her life several times. She tried to find a way to be happy with all her success. But she was miserable. Gina felt like she had to put on a cheerful mask every morning, when she put on her makeup to hide her misery. Despite all her feelings of pain and dissatisfaction, Gina had a hard time making a commitment to take control of her life and go for her bigger vision.

We worked on the essence of what Gina thought made a person successful, and what she really wanted to bring to people through television. Gina finally realized she had gone after someone else's definition of success. It took two years – and a lot of courage – for Gina to shape her career the way she wanted it. When we last spoke, she said she didn't regret a minute that she spent during that time.

Today, Gina is wealthier. She has a rich, meaningful life, but it now has a style that really suits her soul. Her work gives her meaning and truly makes a difference in people's lives.

Are you ready to make a commitment to yourself and leave all the excuses behind? Following is a contract to honor yourself and make the commitment. MAKE TODAY THE FIRST DAY OF LIFE THAT LEADS TO BUILDING SUCCESS ON YOUR OWN TERMS. Fill out the contract. Date and sign it. Make a photocopy of it. Then post your contract where you will see it every day.

If you don't feel comfortable just yet signing the contract, photocopy it and keep it where you can see it every day. Look at the resistance you are having to signing the contract. Ask yourself these three questions.

1. What is holding me back from taking action?

2. Where can I get support to help me succeed?

3. What will it feel like when I sign the contract and take action to create success on my own terms?

---

**Contract for Creating The Soul of Success in My Life**

                                                    Date _____

I, _____, have made a conscious choice to take action and create what I want for my life and my work.

I will take three steps in the next week to get started:
1.
2.
3.

The three most important things for me to accomplish in the next month are:
1.
2.
3.

I am paying attention to what is really important to me and my intention is to bring _____

into my life before _____(month) __ (day) of ___ (year).
I will know I am making progress when

I have selected two people who will support and encourage me without judgment to create success on my own terms. Their names are _____ and _____.

                        Signed_____

---

# Step 2
## Clearing the foundation

*"A mind once stretched by a new idea, never regains its
original dimensions."* ~ Oliver Wendell Holmes

You have gotten conscious about what you want
to create in your life and have made the commitment to
yourself to take action. Reviewing what has worked and
what hasn't worked in your life will be very helpful in
moving forward. If you look for the essence of each event
that brought you success or struggle, you will usually
find one of the two patterns listed below. You'll also find
out what you were feeling and who you were being.

•   *Limiting Beliefs* and *negative thoughts* are usually
    present with undesired outcomes or *STRUGGLES.*

•   *Positive thoughts, collaboration,* and *strategic
    support* are present with desired outcomes and
    *SUCCESSES.*

By examining these recurring threads in your life,
you can see *you* have made the *CHOICES* – consciously
or unconsciously – which led to your results. With
recognition comes personal power to choose and to
change patterns and outcomes. Consciously choosing
your actions allows you to stop repeating the patterns
that don't serve you.

### Case Study: Bringing Self-doubt Out in the Open

Every time Sarah had a bad performance review
or found it difficult to pull together a team, it was
because her "judging voice" would kick in. She realized
this voice came from her uncle. He always told Sarah
that she would never really amount to much. Sarah's
uncle had lived with her for two years when she was 10
years old.

Sarah was a very curious and enterprising child. She was always thinking up ways to earn a little money with small jobs around the neighborhood. When Sarah was excited by the money she had made with her lemonade stand or weeding a neighbor's garden, her uncle would scoff at her efforts. He said she would never have success and it would be smart for her to concentrate on finding a husband when she got old enough.

Overcoming self-doubt was very difficult for Sarah. Intellectually, she could clearly see these doubts. She realized that her inner critic was really getting in her way. However, the inner critic had such power over her. It took a tremendous amount of effort and courage to face her inner critic every day, and not give into it. Brief coaching calls before big presentations and important events kept Sarah focused on desired outcomes and defined results. She used affirmations to keep her mind clear from the constant chatter of her inner critic.

Sarah found that digging to the essence of each struggle took courage and hard work. By looking at what the inner critic was bringing forward, she could take action to move beyond the doubt and the fear.

Once Sarah uncovered the essence of her struggles, she was able to spot the patterns when they started again. We worked on getting clear about the project, developing a strategic approach. Sarah gained support and momentum through collaboration. Six months later, Sarah was promoted to director of her marketing division. She also found that recognizing patterns of self-doubt made her relationships more rewarding.

## ---- Exercise ----

## Discovering Your Patterns with Struggle

Think back over the last two years when you've experienced struggles or setbacks in your career. What were some of the common threads?

Did you have doubts or negative thoughts at the beginning of the situation?

What were some of the feelings and emotions that surfaced?

What was the defining moment of struggle or setback in the situation?

Now that you have identified these patterns, what can you do when you see them starting up again?

What changes in perception or action do you need to make?

What outcome do you really want to create?

--------

### Case Study: Seeing the Value of Your Contributions

Terry had no trouble recognizing the essence of his struggles once we looked into his specific situations; however, he found it much more difficult to uncover the essence of his successes.

I asked Terry to describe the essence of the successes in his life. His first reaction to my question was "There really isn't one." Terry attributed successful projects and jobs to either one of the following two reasons: (1) these events were purely by chance or (2) he was a member of a team, and other people had made it happen.

It is common for my clients to feel stuck with this exercise at first. Some of them can't get to the essence of their successes, because they feel as Terry did. It was all a coincidence or the result of someone else's actions. Other clients can easily list their successes and feel successful, but can't really put their finger on what they do to create their successes.

I asked Terry to describe what a successful project looked like. Then we looked at the last two years to see where he thought the company had been successful. I asked Terry to make a list of all the projects that he had been a part of and regarded as successful. I told him to include every successful outcome that came to mind even if he didn't think he played a part in it.

For each project on the list, we looked at the essence of what made it successful. Then we looked at what Terry's role had been on the project. Terry could see the following pattern emerge: *his strengths and contributions were showing up as an integral part of each project.* By identifying his strengths and contributions on past projects, Terry could work to strengthen and build on these qualities to bring more success into his life.

## PART 1
### Limiting Beliefs: Cracks in the foundation

*"If you can not find peace within yourself, you will never find it anywhere else."* ~ Marvin Gaye

Just as a house needs a strong foundation and will crumble if built on shifting sand, we need a firm foundation with a core that is solid and supple to carry us through a multitude of life experiences and leave us standing and thriving. Some of the foundation we build ourselves, and some is laid by others. Getting to the essence of who you are and what you really want to create in your life takes you back to look at the workmanship of your foundation.

You will need to review if the footings are solid and built on level ground. You will need to chisel off any material that sloughed over the foundation and is no longer necessary. You will need to make sure that the concrete used was of high quality and without many air pockets where structural weakness could set in.

If we don't look at Limiting Beliefs consciously, they can be a crack in our foundation. Become aware of them, reframe them into Expansive Beliefs, and use them as a point of illumination and possibility.

### Case Study: Realizing What No Longer Serves You

Earlier in this chapter, I shared the story of Sarah. Her uncle built part of her foundation. During the two years that he lived with her family, Sarah's uncle laid unnecessary concrete. He planted the seed of doubt and judgment. Because she did not have an objective frame of reference, Sarah nurtured this seed into a Limiting Belief.

Sarah was able to chisel off her uncle's concrete. She reframed the Limiting Belief into a tool for evaluating situations in her life.

Sarah would notice her reaction to a new project or challenge and see if it struck a cord with the old belief. If it did, Sarah knew it was important to do the work collaboratively. She sought out objective support to bounce her ideas off and move forward in confident action. This empowered her to try new challenges and remove any residual power the Limiting Belief had over her.

### What negative energy do you hold about money?

Money is one of the most common areas where we have Limiting Beliefs. During childhood, our parents or people of authority make seemingly small and innocent remarks or actions about it. However, these types of remarks can keep us chained to a negative energy around money.

- "Wash your hands after handling money. It's dirty."
- "Money is the root of all evil."
- "Don't spend your money all in one place."
- "Is it something you need or something you want? Better save your money for the needs."
- "You can't keep that money. You didn't do enough to earn it."

When people said the phrases above they usually weren't saying them consciously. They did not think of how it would affect you or if the words would hurt you. Even so, these remarks had a profound impact on our relationship with money and consequently our lives.

### Case Study: Limiting Beliefs Sabotage Prosperity

When I was growing up, both my parents worked for ABC Sports and traveled a great deal. When my brother (who was three years older than me) and I were very young, they hired a housekeeper to look after us. Once my brother turned 13 years old, my mother left him in charge and we looked after ourselves. Whenever she left home for two days or more, my mother would leave us with a lot of cash – between $800 and $1,000 – in case we needed groceries, cab fare, spending money, etc.

It was only a few years ago that I realized one of my Limiting Beliefs about money stemmed from this habit. I did not want a pocket full of cash. What I really wanted was my mother to be home. I had translated that into the thought that having money meant not having genuine connections with people and loving interaction. For years even though I worked hard and was successful on many levels I subconsciously would never let real wealth flow to me.

My nature is to build strong connections with people and be of service and that Limiting Belief framed them as being mutually exclusive of each other.

### ---- Exercise ----
### The Energy of Money

This exercise will help you get at your Limiting Beliefs around money. Once you recognize your negative or anxious thoughts around money, you can look for ways to improve your relationship with it. An optimistic perspective will attract money more easily into your life.

What are the first three things you think of when you think of money?
1.
2.
3.

What are your thoughts and feelings when you pay your bills?

Do you enjoy buying a gift for yourself or a friend?

Do you place too low a value on the work you do? Is this low value because of a Limiting Belief you hold?

How can you make what you really want and feel worthy of that amount?

When someone gives you a gift, do you say "thank you" and smile? Or do you say things like "Oh, you shouldn't have... it was nothing really"?

Do you feel guilty making too much money? Is there a sense that if you are making too much money, there won't be enough for someone else?

What do you hear yourself thinking and feeling about someone who has a lot of money?

What patterns about money have you had in your life?

Imagine that you were to win a Big Game ticket with an estimated jackpot of $250 million. If you had the winning ticket, do you think of paying off bills, going on vacation, etc.? Or do you think about putting a bigger vision into action like establishing a foundation, starting a business, etc.?

--------

The whole idea of finances, wealth, and prosperity goes way beyond the balance in your checkbook or the numbers in your stock portfolio. *It is a state of mind. A feeling of being connected. A feeling of fulfillment.* If you come from a perspective of scarcity and things being restricted and limited, you will always feel like you don't have enough. If you come from a perspective of abundance, you can effortlessly attract money because you have positive, expansive feelings about it. You focus on what you want in relationship to money and not what you don't want or don't have.

### Case Study: Focusing on the Big Picture

Sheri owned a florist shop. It was the answer to a life long dream of owning a business. Sheri worked hard to save enough money for startup capital and persuaded a bank to loan her the money she needed to open the business.

Sheri was very good at connecting with people. She believed that customer service was the most important service provided by her store. Within nine months of opening her store, Sheri had a large base of regular customers and a steady source of referrals for new business. From the customer's viewpoint, her business appeared to be successful and growing quickly.

Sheri hired me because she was worried about her business. She was barely making a profit. Her customers were very satisfied and always talking up her store, but her financial books showed a very different picture. No matter what she did, revenues just never seemed to grow significantly. Sheri was discouraged and worried she would lose the store if she didn't turn things around fast. She was also exhausted.

We looked at what Limiting Beliefs Sheri had around money and around success. Sheri realized that her idea of success was really her father's. He had always struggled in business as a salesman; he always seemed to have one deal after another blow up on him. Sheri had grown up with a sense that the only way to succeed was to do everything yourself. That way, nobody could wreck your business deals for you. Sheri also discovered that she had taken pieces of her father's fearful attitude about money into her business life.

I asked Sheri to think about what was important to her and what she really wanted her business to bring into her life. She wanted the challenge and satisfaction of owning her own business. Sheri said she wanted to generate large profits so she could travel and have financial security without having to work all of the time.

We developed a business model that had Sheri working "on" her business instead of "in" her business. She came up with systems on how she liked everything to be done.

She talked to some colleagues and found an excellent bookkeeper to keep everything organized and take that huge task off her shoulders.

Sheri used the time freed up from bookkeeping to develop her marketing plan, which identified four key revenue streams to incorporate into the business. She hired some part-time help while she started putting the new systems into place.

With just these few changes, Sheri was able to increase her profits over the next two months. Revenues still needed to increase before she could reach her goals but the changes were creating momentum. Sheri's renewed excitement made the work seem effortless.

Sheri reframed her Limiting Beliefs about success and money, turning them into valuable tools. She used these tools get clear to stay focused. Sheri used the tools

to hire people who shared her Expansive Beliefs of
success and money.

#### ---- Exercise ----
### Shifting Limiting Beliefs to Expansive Beliefs

Because Limiting Beliefs can have such a powerful negative
effect on our lives is very important to be able to recognize
them and reframe them into Expansive Beliefs. Expansive
Beliefs become powerful tools in moving us forward. This four-
part exercise will help you begin to reframe Limiting Beliefs into
Expansive Beliefs.

1.  Using your journal, notebook, or computer file, spend a few
    minutes answering the following questions:

    -   What assumptions do you make about people or events
        before they occur?
    -   What are the recurring patterns in your life?
    -   What feelings are central to these patterns?
    -   What underlying beliefs do you hold that continue to
        create these patterns?
    -   What do you believe that friends, colleagues or family
        always do to you?

2.  Make a list of strong opinions and beliefs that you have.

    Examples:
    -   "I'm not smart enough to..."
    -   "Rich people are ruthless..."
    -   "All men are jerks..."
    -   "I can't speak in front of a crowd, because they may
        think..."
    -   "I can't apply for that position, because I can't..."
    -   "No one would pay me that kind of money..."
    -   "I will never lose weight because..."
    -   "I'm not creative enough to..."

3.  Review your list and identify the Limiting Beliefs.

4. On a new sheet of paper in your journal or notebook, draw a line straight down the center of the page. Write "Limiting Beliefs" on the left side of the page. Write "Expansive Beliefs" on the right side of the page.

**Example:**

| Limiting Beliefs | Expansive Beliefs |
|---|---|

- In the left-hand column under the "Limiting Beliefs" heading:
  (1) Write down one of the Limiting Beliefs from your list.
  (2) Write down the evidence you have that it is true.
  (3) Complete (1) and (2) for each of your Limiting Beliefs.

- In the right-hand column under the "Expansive Belief" heading:
  (1) Describe how you would reframe your first Limiting Belief in the left-hand column into an Expansive Belief.
  (2) Write down evidence you already know or would need to support this Expansive Belief.
  (3) Complete (1) and (2) for each of your Limiting Beliefs.

**Example:**

| Limiting Beliefs | Expansive Beliefs |
|---|---|
| *Limiting Belief: I'm not ready to expand my client base yet.*<br><br>*Evidence: I don't have all of the answers.* | *Expansive Belief: I have experience in a lot of areas. I can continue to learn as I expand my business.*<br><br>*Evidence: My current clients are making lots of progress and give me unsolicited feedback on the tremendous value they receive working with me.* |

TIPS FOR REFRAMING LIMITING BELIEFS: For each Limiting Belief, ask yourself the following questions to help you reframe it:

- Who first told me this?
- Who says it to me now?
- What stops me?
- What evidence makes this true?

These questions will help you open to a new perspective. They will create a new awareness of your choices and possibilities available as you change things in your life.

--------

### You create your perspective

Our thoughts are very powerful.  They create the lens that we use to view our life experiences through. When our Limiting Beliefs are smeared on our glasses of life, we have a distorted view that makes it very hard to see clearly.

Because we have been looking out of this same pair of glasses for most of our lives, we think our perception is correct. We base our actions and reactions on what we think is accurate information. However it's not accurate at all.

Our Limiting Beliefs are built upon things that are no longer true and probably never were.  We have gotten so used to them – and spent so much of our lives trying to continually find new evidence to support them – that we have lost all perspective of what is true for us.

We can clear off our glasses and quickly retrain our brains to see the clear focused perspective that is our true nature by looking for evidence to support our Expansive Beliefs.

#### ---- Exercise ----

## The Little Gems Notebook

Please buy one 3" x 2" spiral-bound memo book. It should either open like a book or flip open from the top.  This memo book is available in any grocery or stationary store in the school supplies section.

Carry this small memo book around with you everywhere! Use it to write down the "Little Gems" that people give you throughout the day. What are Little Gems? They are wonderful gifts of words, smiles, praise, positive feedback, a good feeling, etc. We seldom hear, accept or acknowledge these Little Gems. However, people share them with you each day. You may even share them with yourself. Following are examples of Little Gems:

- Someone says, "I liked your idea about the new project."
- You think, "I did a good job with that..."
- Someone says, "You really did a good job with that introduction at the meeting..."
- Someone smiles a friendly smile.

Put your ATTENTION on what people are really saying to you. Make it your INTENTION to really hear them and to acknowledge and accept the positive messages. Make sure to capture the ones that you give yourself no matter how small. It won't take you long at all to fill up your Little Gem book. Several times a day, you should stop to jot down the gems – especially those that you couldn't write down right away. They represent powerful evidence to support your Expansive Beliefs, which will move you forward and build the momentum of your success.
Imagine that every smile, kind word or genuine connection is someone giving you a lovely flower. If you don't accept these gems, it's like throwing the flower on the floor. Pretty rude, don't you think? So just smile and continue with your day.

--------

### Case Study: Some People's Gem Books Fill Up Faster Than Others

Lauren was surprised how quickly her Little Gem book filled up. Three times every day, she took two minutes to jot down the kind words that people said. She also captured the little positive energy moments like a smile...the man that let her go in front of him in line...a woman who paid for her toll.

Lauren noticed the more she became aware of these gem moments, the more of them she had. She found herself being less judgmental of herself and others. Her days became more fun. Even when she encountered challenging situations at the office, Lauren seemed to work through them more easily.

Noticing her Limiting Beliefs and being aware when her fears or resistance to a situation were triggered by these beliefs allowed Lauren to remove the power they had over her. She looked at the old evidence to prove the Limiting Belief was true. She found no evidence just harmful self-doubt added to negative events in her life. Creating Expansive Beliefs from her Limiting Beliefs allowed Lauren to remove struggle and fear from her life and gave her a sense of exhilaration.

If you have a heavy shell of skepticism or self-doubt, it may take you a little longer to fill up your gem book. Once you actively look for Little Gems in words, acts, emotions or gestures, you will notice them showing up more frequently.

The power of a smile is magical. A funny thing happens when you notice the Little Gems that people give: *you find yourself consciously smiling in return.* As you acknowledge these gifts, you give them back and your whole outlook shifts. This shift in perspective changes the way people perceive you and the momentum of Little Gems accelerates. You feel lighter and you attract more gifts into your life.

Remember, if you don't think you will find many Little Gems to write down, be patient. Be aware. Graciously accept the ones you notice; build your momentum and fill your little book.

*Are you ready to let go of your Limiting Beliefs and turn them in for Expansive Beliefs?*

## PART 2

## Your story: A saga used as a crutch or a powerful leveraging tool

*"Wisdom is knowing what to do next, skill is knowing how to do it, and virtue is doing it." ~ David Starr Jordan*

*"The boat isn't steered by its wake."* This phrase was used by one of my teleclass leaders at Coach U to make us think about our life story and the things that had gone before but were keeping us stuck.

We tend to look at our personal history as a road map for our future under the false impression that past success or failure is an indicator of more of the same in the future. The character of the wake is determined by the boat's speed, direction, and impact on the water; the wake has no influence over the boat's speed, direction and impact.

This is true with our personal history, as well. We all have a unique story that has shaped and strengthened us. It has perfected our gifts. The trick is to use our story as leverage to personal achievement – not as an excuse that limits our vision and prescribes an outcome of struggle or failure.

*What is your story?* Are you using it to support your Limiting Beliefs and make struggle the status quo? Or are you proud of your story (painful though it may be in some of chapters) and looking at all the gifts your story has provided you with?

Before you can decipher your story, you need to change your perspective. You need to *know* the wake does not drive the boat, and your story does not drive you. Everything that has happened in your life has culminated in the exceptional person that you are right now! It has brought you here to the time of choosing to come to consciousness and choosing to begin your true journey in earnest.

---- **Exercise** ----

## Finding the Essence of How Your Story Has Served You

Look back at your list of Limiting Beliefs. Choose two that have had the most powerful impact on your life.

1.    On a new sheet of paper in your journal, notebook, or computer file, write about the first of these two Limiting Beliefs:

       • Describe what took place and when you first experienced this Limiting Belief.

       • Write two other times that stand out when you or someone else reinforced this Limiting Belief.

2.    Now write about the second of your two Limiting Beliefs.

3.    Review what you have written about your Limiting Beliefs. Answer the following questions, which will help reveal how your story has served you:

       • If the event was painful, did it make you more aware of your surroundings? Did it help you evaluate what is important to you? Did you then decide on the best actions for you to take?

       • If you suffered a lot of judgment, did you understand the powerful negative consequences of judging? Did you use these feelings to be more perceptive and compassionate?

       • If you were told you were unworthy, has that been a catalyst for you to strive to do your best and reach out to other people to help them be their best?

The power of this exercise is twofold. You reframe your Limiting Beliefs into Expansive Beliefs, while also using the essence of your story as a springboard for new possibilities.

--------

Have you been using your Limiting Beliefs and the rough patches in your personal story to keep your life involuntary? Does your mind take a shallow breath of Limiting Beliefs? Or does your mind take a deep conscious breath and explore the situation before forming opinions or making decisions?

### *Case Study: Taking Some Space to Look at Your Life*

Julie was committed to making conscious choices and changes in her life. She wanted more out of her business and she wanted to put more fun in her life. Even with her desire for change, she was still coming up with a lot of struggle. We worked on identifying and reframing her Limiting Beliefs. We examined what things in her story might be responsible for holding her back and creating the struggle she was feeling.

Julie could not understand how the unpleasant parts of her life story had been of service to her. She didn't see how they could possibly help her move forward. She could see how her successes were good examples to help build her confidence and identify her strengths. However, the mundane and difficult parts of her story outnumbered the successes. When it came to those parts of her past, she was finding it hard to turn off her shallow thinking and breathing. Julie had planned to take one week of vacation. I suggested she use that time as an opportunity to have a "conscious day." She joked about how she might need to take a vacation after her vacation. Staying conscious and in tune with what was going on every minute of the day had been a hard exercise for her when I asked her to do it for one day. Julie thought that staying conscious for one week – every minute of the day – would be almost impossible.

During our next phone call, Julie sounded energized and excited. In a delighted voice, she said to me, "I feel like I'm finally awake!" Her vacation had been wonderful. After the first day being aware of her thoughts, feelings, and choices of how to react, Julie found having a conscious day effortless. She found that most of her struggle was because she was not focusing on what she wanted. Instead, she had been focusing on what wasn't working and how long it was taking to change.

By reflecting on her story, Julie realized that she had been doing this most of her life. It was the cause of her dissatisfaction and struggle. Julie was able to clearly see that the patterns of the past were holding her back. She was ready to make deliberate choices instead of reactions. But Julie was still unclear how the difficult parts of her story had served her.

I asked her to think of three times in her life that she remembered as being very difficult and what they had in common.

After a long pause, Julie said, "They taught me not to give up." The boring and routine times had taught Julie to look at details and become more precise. This new perspective allowed Julie to focus on what she wanted and move forward without so much struggle and hesitation.

#### ---- Exercise ----

### Pulling Your Strengths from Your Story

### Talents + Knowledge + Experiential Skill = Strengths

A talent or strength can be easily overlooked, because it comes so naturally to you. Discovering your talents and honing them by adding knowledge and experiential skills will move you from strong to superb.

- A TALENT is something that comes easily to you – a natural way of doing, feeling, thinking or reacting to things. When you add knowledge and skill, you perfect this talent into a STRENGTH.

- A STRENGTH is something that you use over and over in different situations and applications to achieve high levels of success with ease and predictably.

Write down what you think are your top five greatest strengths:
1.
2.
3.
4.
5.

Think of things that friends or colleagues always say about your actions. Examples: "You are so good at organizing events." "Networking and making connections with people is so easy for you." "You have an incredible ability to have confidence in the outcomes of projects."

Write down three situations in which people have made remarks to you that are similar to the examples above:
1.
2.
3.

--------

**--- Exercise ----**

## How to Describe Your Strengths with Precise Language

The next step in identifying your strengths is getting to the essence of your natural style of doing things and putting precise language around what your strengths are.

EXAMPLE:

You have just been brought in to head a new division. You know what the company wants to accomplish and your job is to make it happen. You love this kind of challenge.

What strengths make you love this challenge (i.e. people skills, organizational skills, etc.)? To identify the essence of your strength, you need to look deeper and be more precise.

- *Is your strength strategic thinking?* You can look at the objectives of the company and immediately develop a broad strategy of meeting those objectives. You can look ahead and anticipate new strategies to meet the company's objectives.

OR

- *Is your strength creative-process thinking?* You look at the objectives of the company. Within your new division, you can clearly see what systems, tools, and structures need to be put into place to effectively carry out those objectives.

These strengths seem similar; however, they are very different when you look at them in action.

- The STRATEGIC THINKER has a bigger vision. This individual can look at "what-if's" and try different angles, but is bogged down by details and systems.

- The CREATIVE THINKER likes a closer view of the picture, creating the systems and tools to carry things out. This individual feels overwhelmed and unfocused, if he or she has to look at too broad of a picture.

--------

Getting to the essence and using precise language will eliminate struggle and leverage your strengths into success. Developing the skill to spot the talents of other people – and help them build their strengths – will help you become a more effective entrepreneur, manager, and leader.

### Case Study: Capitalizing on Your Strengths

Lori wasn't sure what her strengths were. She was good with people and liked things organized but she didn't see those as things she could capitalize on to build her career. I asked her to use precise language to describe thoughts, feelings, and actions that came to her naturally in a situation she would describe as being "good with people."

Lori said, "People find it easy to talk to me; I seem to calm them down. I also enjoy working with all kinds of personalities; I'm even good with difficult people." Active listening and strong personal boundaries were two key strengths Lori was able to identify.

We went to the essence of these two strengths. After sharing several specific examples, Lori could see a pattern emerge.

She was very good at listening and mirroring back what she heard the customer say to make sure she understood correctly.

Lori was good at setting boundaries and not taking things personally; this allowed her to listen to customer complaints and find satisfactory solutions. This talent was also very helpful in dealing with two of her supervisors who had a reputation for being "difficult to work with."

Her natural talents for organization and creating systems allowed her to follow through on staffing requirements and track possible inefficiencies and correct them before errors were made.

Lori worked on clearly identifying and labeling her talents. We developed strategies to add knowledge and practical skill resulting in five highly developed strengths:

1. Active listening
2. Clear communication
3. Strong personal boundaries
4. Strategic thinking
5. Organization

Once she was able to clearly define these five strengths, we worked on ways to leverage them to create an opportunity for her to get a promotion that gave her tremendous job satisfaction and an excellent salary.

Setting boundaries is a way to clearly define what you will allow to happen in a conversation or interaction. You can either tell people your boundaries or show them your boundaries by controlling the interaction.

## PART 3

## Is your head still looking back while your body is facing forward?

*"Imagination is the beginning of creation.
You imagine what you desire; you will what you imagine;
and at last you create what you will."*
~ *George Bernard Shaw*

The next step in your journey is to begin to create want you really want in your life and career. However, before you move forward to Step 3, ask yourself the following questions:

- Are you breathing and thinking on purpose...or is it still involuntary?

- Have you stopped and cleared all of the pebbles from your shoe...or is there still one that's rolled to the toe and currently out of mind?

- Have you chiseled all of the unnecessary concrete from your foundation... or are there still a few sharp pieces that need to be excavated?

- Who is driving the boat – you or the wake?

One of the troubles with Limiting Beliefs and inner critic voices from our life story is that we've been wearing them for a very long time. They're like a pair of comfortable old sneakers.

We're used to them and although they may be ragged and the leather too soft to support us properly they are familiar and easy to slip into.

Wouldn't it be better to keep the pair we have and not risk all the time and effort looking for the ultimate style and then breaking them in? That's a question you need to consciously answer about getting to the *soul of success* in your life.

It is only natural that making changes in your life would cause some doubt and discomfort. The passion and pain exercise revealed you are either in enough discomfort to motivate your moving forward or you have become numb to the discomfort because of your state of overwhelm.

Either way, it's really not comfortable wearing that old pair of sneakers. When you travel down fresh paths, gaps in the sole let in pebbles and sticks. Small puddles feel like lakes, as water seeps in and soaks your socks.

Getting conscious takes courage. Actively taking deep oxygen rich breathes takes focus. Chiseling off extra material from our foundation takes elbow grease. But it's a choice we need to make.

It's all about choice; stay where we are and complain about how we want it to be different... or roll up our sleeves and make it different.

### A powerful tool to transform Limiting Beliefs

The 90 / 10 Rule is a powerful tool to reframe Limiting Beliefs into Expansive Beliefs. In addition to enhancing where you are right now, this tool can perform as a springboard to your success.

The 90 / 10 Rule states that 10% of life is made up of what happens to you; 90% of life is decided by how you react.

In other words, 10 % of what happens is not in our circle of control. We can't stop the plane from being late, which makes us rush for our next connection. We can't alter the heavy flow of traffic, which makes us late for our appointment.

We do not have control of this 10 % of life that occurs. BUT we do have control over the ensuing 90 % of life, by consciously choosing our actions instead of just having a reaction.

Example:
        You're sitting eating breakfast. Your daughter and puppy are playing. The puppy slips on the rug and bumps the table, which spills your juice on your outfit. You yell at the puppy, which scares him and he piddles on the rug. Your daughter starts crying because you've frightened her and the puppy. Your husband gets mad because you tell him to clean up the mess because changing your clothes is going to make you late.
        You're on a roll now! Muttering to yourself as you change your clothes and rush to get into your car; you knock over the window box that you and your daughter planted last weekend. Then you rush off to work. Since you are still reacting, things just continue to go down hill. When you pick your daughter up after work, she won't talk to you. She won't let you say "hi" to the puppy, because she's afraid you'll scare him again. *Ugh!*

        Let's rewind the day's events in this example. What caused the bad day?
A.  Did the juice cause it?
B.  Did the puppy cause it?
C.  Did your daughter cause it?
D.  Did you cause it?

        The answer is D. *You caused the bad day!* The juice spilling – which started off the whole chain of events – was something out of your circle of control. It was the 10% of what happened in the day. How you chose to react set in motion the other 90% of the day that followed.
        Remember: Even if you don't consciously choose something, you are still making a choice. And things will flow from that choice.
        In the juice example, what conscious choices could you have made that would have given you a different outcome?
        Return to the moment that the juice spills. Don't react, *choose* your actions. Quickly grab a towel to wipe up the spill. Then corral the puppy and your daughter,

and set some rules for indoor play and outdoor play. Ask if they want to come up and help you choose a blouse to replace the one with the little juice stain. In five minutes, you're on your way and the day is looking up.

*Same start to the day. But very different outcomes.*

You made the difference in how the day turned out. Consciously choosing your actions altered the flow of what you brought into your day.

### --- Exercise ----

### Practicing The 90 / 10 Rule

I would like you to spend the next three days consciously practicing The 90 / 10 Rule. Look at everything that happens in your day. Identify the 10 % you have no control over and the 90 % you do. Choose your actions and take steps to create the outcomes you want.

In your journal, notebook or computer file, write down three examples of how an outcome changed because you were using The 90 / 10 Rule. Describe what was valuable about the new outcomes.

1.
2.
3.

--------

Why is concentrating on becoming conscious and making choices – *rather than simply making decisions* – so important?

What is so important about recognizing your Limiting Beliefs and the power of your personal story? Because they are what stands between you and the soul of your success!

From the Gallup organization to Yale University and Harvard Business School, researchers from a variety of groups and institutions have examined what successful people have in common. From their studies, the following themes have consistently emerged:

SUCCESSFUL INDIVIDUALS...

1.    Demonstrate a willingness and ability to clear away the physical and emotional disorder that lies in the path of their success.

2.    Take deliberate action – even during setbacks – to create momentum to pull themselves forward.

I would like to share a wonderful quote that inspired me to let my brilliance shine. It has been a powerful tool to help my clients stop hiding behind self-doubt and a misguided sense of humility and step into the power of their own greatness.

*Our deepest fear is not that we are inadequate.*
*Our deepest fear is that we are powerful beyond measure.*
*It is our light, not our darkness, that most frightens us.*
*We ask ourselves, who am I to be brilliant,*
*gorgeous, talented and fabulous?*

*Actually, who are you not to be?*
*You are a child of God. Your playing small*
*does not serve the world. There's nothing enlightened about*
*shrinking so that other people won't feel insecure around you.*
*We are all meant to shine, as children do.*

*We were born to make manifest the glory of God*
*that is within us. It's not just in some of us; it's in everyone.*
*And as we let our own light shine, we unconsciously give other*
*people permission to do the same. As we're liberated from our*
*own fear, our presence automatically liberates others."*

*~ Marianne Williamson, 1992*

Take a deep breath and turn to Step 3. It's time to make your choices and take action!

# Step 3

## Following Your Inner Compass

*"What lies behind us, and what lies before us
are tiny matters compared to what lies within us."*
~ *Ralph Waldo Emerson*

*NOW is the only real moment you can affect in your life!*

"The past is history. The future's a mystery. The
present is perfect...that's why they call it a gift." So why
do we spend so much time ruminating over could-a,
should-a, would-a's? We worry or plan for the future
and spend little if any time thinking about RIGHT NOW.

I believe this thinking may exist in part for two
reasons: we received this modeling as children and we
live in fast-paced world. Humans naturally strive to
improve and move forward with the current of change.
Change is good as long as we don't loose ourselves in the
rush of the changing tides and rapid flow of the water
through life.

I don't believe you need to change and become
someone better. You don't need to improve and become
someone different than you already are. I believe you
need to shed the extra layers that no longer serve you.
These layers were given to you by someone or you
covered yourself with them. You must uncover who you
really are, what is really important to you, and what you
want to bring to the world.

It's an very important perspective to ponder much
like how Leonardo DaVinci could look at a piece of stone
and see the sculpture within...peeling away the layers
and polishing until the magnificent inner core emerged.
You, too, have the power and creativity to reveal your
inner core... polishing to reveal your unique brilliance.

This means you already have the talents and a
powerful inner compass to fill your soul and fire your
creativity.

Oliver Wendell Holmes said, "Most of us go to our graves with our music still inside us."

*What song do you feel compelled to sing?*

## Tapping Into Your Inner Compass

### Awareness + Acceptance + Action = Momentum

**Awareness:**   Quiet the relentless script that plays repeatedly in your mind.

**Acceptance:**   Release your resistance. Trust that you are exactly where you are supposed to be.

**Action:**   Listen to the soft quiet voice that gives you counsel, guidance, and inspiration. *Then act on it.*

**Momentum:**   Leverage all of your thoughts, feelings, movements, and progress to break your inertia and build momentum.

### *Case Study: Become Aware of Your Toxic Inner Critic*

Joni had a great sense of humor, a fabulous smile, and a passion for bringing together just the right people for a project or special event. Her colleagues would describe her as confident, knowledgeable, and very talented in networking and project planning. However, Joni didn't feel she possessed any of these qualities. Her self-doubt was seriously affecting her life.

One of the first things I asked Joni to do was to become acutely aware of what her inner script or "inner critic" was saying repeatedly to her every day.

I asked her to consciously listen to the loudest, most pointed barbs of the day and write them down. *"You don't really know what you're doing; this time, they'll discover you're a fraud." "Don't tell Sue about your article; it's not that great and she probably won't care."*

*"That's probably someone calling to tell you what a bad job you did on the Peterson layout."*
Joni was surprised at the number of poisonous thoughts she had written down during the course of the day. One of the requirements of her job was speaking on the phone. However, she hated the incoming calls. She recognized why she always jumped a little and hesitated before answering the phone; her inner critic would make up a story that the person on the other end was going to complain or tell her that she was not good enough.

Writing down one week's worth of this relentless script made Joni aware of the tremendous energy drain on her. She could see how this tape constantly eroded her confidence and pleasure in her work.

Joni accepted that these scripts were not her true thoughts. She worked on removing these negative thoughts from her mind. She actively listened to her true inner voice. She listened when it warned her of an unhealthy situation. She listened when moved to try something new. She listened and acted on the breath of inspiration instead of standing in its way.

By tapping into her inner compass, Joni had the momentum needed to remove old thought and behavioral layers. She was able to polish off her authentic self.

### Your thoughts: Powerful tool or destructive force

Did you ever try the experiment of using a magnifying glass with the sun and paper to make fire when you were a child? Remember the power that small amount of light had to ignite the paper!

Your thoughts have even more power. Your thoughts ignite your actions and your life. Your outcomes mirror the quality of your thoughts:

- *Focused affirmative thoughts* give you CONFIDENCE, a sense of purpose. This sense of purpose makes you very attractive to opportunities and results.

- *Swirling negative thoughts* create CONFUSION. This confusion erodes your confidence. It sends mixed signals to the people and opportunities you want to attract into your life.

Have you noticed that a situation or conversation will turn out the way you imagine *before* it happened? If your thoughts are positive and you visualize all going well, everything turns out positive with multiple possibilities. If you thought of all the possible pitfalls, the situation or conversation probably falls into many of those pitfalls. Why? The power of your thoughts directs your attention and actions.

What percentage of your thoughts are negative? It is 10%, 20%, 65% or more?

How many books, audio programs or workshops have you experienced that touched on the idea of how powerful your thoughts are?

People, events and situations do not control your thoughts. They are all external. YOU control your thoughts. Whether you choose thoughts that empower or limit is entirely up to you! It is not a result of external stimulus.

What benefit do you get from letting negative thoughts direct your actions? It isn't easy to be aware of your thoughts – and focus exclusively on the ones that will build momentum and move you forward. However, it's the key to your success.

What strategy can you put into place to become more aware – and improve the quality – of your thoughts?

### Case Study: If You Want Different Results, You Need To Do Things Differently

I first met Lauren four years ago at a chamber of commerce dinner. She had a small consulting business and was dissatisfied with the amount of money she made and the quality of her clients. She also had powerful negative thoughts on just about every subject.

At the time, I was marketing director for a trade show and invited Lauren to participate. She filled out an application. Almost immediately after she signed up,

Lauren started to call me with negative remarks about the upcoming event.

Two weeks was all I could stand. I suggested we grab a cup of coffee to talk about her business and things she wanted to do to make it grow. Lauren had great ideas for expanding her business. However, she admitted that her negative thoughts always sabotaged her efforts. Lauren was very excited after our meeting. She told me this time her business was really going to work.

One year later, I was speaking at a "Woman in Business" discussion panel and ran into Lauren. She said the past year had not gone well. She was very frustrated. Lauren asked if I had a half hour to talk about her business and share some insights on how to help her generate more revenue. We had a good discussion and Lauren left with enthusiasm and new ideas.

Two years later, Lauren called and asked me to coach her. She was tired of just getting by. She wanted to make her business a success. Lauren outlined the different strategies – none of which seemed to have worked – she had used to build momentum and gain clients.

I asked her what she thought was the essence of the struggle around growing her business. She said, "I'm not sure. I have tried just about everything... but I always get the same poor results." I asked if she thought the things she tried – including her approach and outlook – had been different each time.

After a very long pause, Lauren said a few of the ideas had been different. However, her approach and outlook had been the same each time: *Negative.*

It's been 12 months – and a lot of hard work – but Lauren has started to make progress retraining her thoughts. She has gotten very clear about what she wants her business to do for her. She has developed a business model that focuses on working "on" her business – not just "in" her business. Her thoughts are much more positive and she uses them as a powerful tool to move her forward.

When a negative thought occurs, Lauren looks at the essence of it. She looks to see if there is something valuable in the thought – or she just needs to let it go.

## PART 1

### You can't focus on your success If you can't breathe

*"Your words create what you speak about.*
*Learn to speak positively."*
*~ Sanya Roman*

When you need air, your lungs scream and you pay attention. *It's the same feeling with freedom, praise, and happiness.* These three things are needs, and your being is screaming for you to pay attention.

I would like you to take a deep breath. Take another deep breath and hold it. Hold your nose closed with your thumb and forefinger, and just relax without breathing. See how long you can go without taking another breath. While holding your breath, focus on what would make you successful. Breathe normally and answer the following questions:

- After the first 20 seconds, was it harder for you to hold your breath?

- While holding your breath, were you able to focus on what would make you successful?

- After holding your breath for 45 seconds, what was the most urgent thing that your brain wanted to focus on?
   In order to survive, we need air to breathe.
Unless you are excellent at holding your breath for long periods, you had a similar experience to most people who try this exercise. After 45-55 seconds, you had difficulty focusing on success or anything else except for getting

your need for air met.

As you look to create success on your own terms; it's vital for you to understand having unmet personal needs will make it almost impossible to clearly focus on what is important to you.

The need for air is obvious and immediate. Other personal needs are just as vital to our health and success. However, they're not always as acute and easily identified. If our personal needs that affect our thoughts, feelings, and emotions go unmet, our focus will be scattered. We will react from a need rather than act from choice.

Any or all of the following feelings may be signs that your personal needs aren't being met: struggle, frustration, irritability, anger, being unloved or unappreciated. Remember how you needed to get air a few minutes go? Our needs are very powerful; we will do strange things consciously – and unconsciously – in an attempt to get our needs met. The need must be met even if some of those things lead to our own detriment.

Your inner compass will help you get your needs met. Use the formula of **Awareness + Acceptance + Action.** It will help you identify and become aware of your needs. You'll accept that you must take steps – *and take action* – to get these needs met. Otherwise, they will keep getting in your way.

Use your inner compass to design an effective system to dissolve the power that your needs have over you. Cut off the fuel these needs give to your inner critic. *And get these needs met permanently.*

### Case Study: Meet Your Needs and Fulfill Your Dreams

Melanie had a strong need for independence. When this need was met, she was very creative and did her best work. However, Melanie had a boss who micro-managed everyone in the department. He watched her every move. He never gave her the opportunity to do her work without looking over her shoulder. The situation was intolerable. Melanie was moody and irritable. She found herself complaining to her co-workers. By tapping into her inner compass, Melanie was able to meet her need for independence. It allowed her to excel and develop the confidence needed to fulfill a lifelong dream of owning her own company.

Melanie's best friend worked at the same company. She had a need for clarity and support. She worked well under the supervision of Melanie's old boss.

These two contrasting case studies illustrate that one need isn't better than another or more important. *It just is.* Our personal needs are like the need to breathe; we must find healthy, expansive ways to get our personal needs met.

#### ---- Exercise ----

### Needs Assessment

*Identify Your Top Five Needs*

Read the following condensed list of needs. Circle five words that ring true as a NEED for you.

You are looking for a NEED – not a "want," "should" or something external. *A NEED is vital for you to feel whole and be your best.* Be willing to look at the list and try on each of the words. Do not sensor the words you circle. Write down a word that resonates with you – even if you don't think it could possibly be a need. There is significance in that resonance; you may have discovered a hidden need.

| | | |
|---|---|---|
| Abundance | Cooperation | Popularity |
| Acceptance | Encouragement | Power |
| Accomplishment | Enjoyment | Praise |
| Acknowledgement | Excitement | Profitability |
| Appreciation | Forgiveness | Purpose |
| Approval | Freedom | Recognition |
| Attention | Friendships | Respect |
| Autonomy | Fulfillment | Security |
| Balance | Fun | Self-respect |
| Belonging | Honesty | Sincerity |
| Calmness | Humor | Stability |
| Caring | Importance | Stillness |
| Challenge | Independence | To be appreciated |
| Change | Influence | To be cared about |

| Clarity | Knowledge | To contribute |
|---|---|---|
| Comfort | Leisure | To be heard |
| Commitments | Loyalty | To be liked |
| Communication | Order | To be loved |
| Compliments | Perfection | To be needed |
| Connections | Permission | To be right |
| Control | | To be valued |

*Prioritize Your Top Five Needs*

Fill in the chart following these steps; leave shaded squares blank.

1. In the TOP ROW of boxes, write your five needs in any order.
2. In the FAR LEFT COLUMN, write your five needs in the same order as the top row. (Refer to sample chart provided later in this section.)
3. Compare the need in the TOP BOX OF THE LEFT COLUMN with the FIRST BOX OF THE TOP ROW. Which one do you need most? *If one need seems to fit under the umbrella of another, choose the one that is larger.* Following across and down on the grid, write down the most important of the two needs in the first available open square.
4. Continue this process until you've filled in all the open squares.
5. Count how many times you wrote each need in the grid. On the lines underneath the grid, write down the need with the number next to it. (Note: When the numbers are added together, the total amount should be equal to 10.)

**Your Needs Assessment Chart**

**SAMPLE**

**Needs Assessment Chart**

| | Freedom | To be liked | Comfort | Excitement | Influence |
|---|---|---|---|---|---|
| Freedom | | Freedom | Freedom | Excitement | Freedom |
| To be liked | | | To be liked | Excitement | Influence |
| Comfort | | | | Excitement | Influence |
| Excitement | | | | | Excitement |

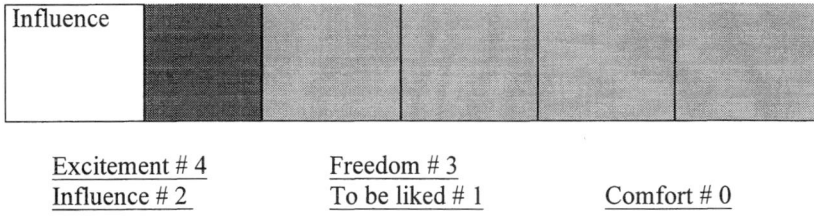

| Influence |
|-----------|

Excitement # 4          Freedom # 3
Influence # 2           To be liked # 1          Comfort # 0

**---- Exercise ----**

## Getting Your Needs Met

Ask yourself the following questions about each need identified in your Needs Assessment Chart:

- What is so important to you about getting this need met?
- How do you feel when this need is getting met?
- How do you behave?
- How does it change your day?
- How do you feel when this need is not getting met?
- How do you behave?
- How does it change your day?

After identifying your needs and what makes them so powerful, what strategies can you develop to meet these needs? You can develop and implement these strategies by yourself or with the help of another person. Use clear, direct language if you're asking another person to help you. He or she will better understand exactly how to fill that need. Start with an "I" statement that clearly defines what you want. Then begin with "Will you" and make a direct request of the other person.

Write down three things you can do to meet your needs:
1.
2.
3.

Write down three requests that someone could do or say to fill
your need:

1.

2.

3.

--------

## Case Study: Identifying All Your Unmet Needs

The first time we worked through the "Needs
Assessment" exercise, it was very difficult for Terry to
narrow the list down to just five top needs. He had a
strong reaction to 30 words. If these 30 needs were not
met, Terry felt it would really stand in his way.

Terry was finally able to select the biggest needs –
the ones that were giving him the most frustration and
struggle when they weren't met.

After he worked through the exercise, we came up
with several strategies for getting these top five needs
met. Terry asked his brother to help him work on one.
A friend was able to help him address another. He was
able to meet the remaining three needs by himself,
making some shifts with boundaries and expectations.

Terry's feelings of struggle diminished, but he was
still frustrated. Over the next seven months, I asked
Terry to work on the "Needs Assessment" exercise three
more times. Each time, Terry identified new needs and
strategies for getting them met in healthy ways.

Remember: Just like our need to breathe, we
must get our emotional needs met. Otherwise, we
cannot focus on what we want and be our best. It is
possible to get your needs permanently met. Every year,
review your "Needs Assessment" twice. Use the exercise
to identify any new needs that are keeping you from
being your best.

### Case Study: Discovering a Hidden Need Removes Struggle

Sarah's top five needs were excitement, freedom, influence, to be liked, and comfort. She was surprised that excitement and freedom made her list – and intrigued when they showed up on her "Needs Assessment Chart" as #1 and #2. Sarah had thought her top two needs would have been comfort and to be needed.

Sarah could see that when these two needs were met, she enjoyed her job and was very productive. When these two needs were met in her relationships, Sarah found that talking, sharing, and just being with someone was effortless. Awareness and making conscious choices helped Sarah permanently meet these needs.

Moving to the next step and completing the "Values assessment exercise" really built Sarah's momentum. She began creating her life by choice instead of just getting by.

The nautical compass is one of man's most important tools. This invention changed the world. It permitted the expansion of global trade routes, while providing sailors with a more secure and reliable method of navigating the seas throughout the year. With the compass, sailors were no longer limited to traveling in summer months when the skies were clear and bird migrations more frequent.

We all come into the world with an inner compass. *This innate gift is your most powerful tool.* We need to acknowledge this gift. We must use our inner compass to keep the blade of this powerful tool sharp.

# PART 2

## Adjust your inner magnet of appeal

*"I need to take an emotional breath, step back, and remind myself who's actually in charge of my life."*
~ *Judith M. Knowlton*

The full power of your inner compass is unleashed when you use your values to set your course. Each of us has a set of inner values. They are not based on morals or social factors; they are at the core of our authentic selves. Our inner values are a strategic tool to remind us of our true nature and life purpose – a rudder to steer our course. Our values help us create our lives on purpose and our success by design.

### Case Study: Breaking Through Reluctance and Inertia has Many Rewards

Elise was very reluctant to fill out the "Values Assessment" exercise. She felt tremendous resistance even though completing her "Needs Assessment" had been very valuable in moving her forward.

After three weeks of procrastinating, Elise used our next coaching call to finish the "Values Assessment." She was very surprised by what the exercise revealed were her top five values; some things that she thought were important to her only ranked #9 and #10.

Integrity and freedom were Elise's #1 and #2 values. She discovered these values were not evident in her work or relationships with friends and family. Elise created a personal definition. This personal definition included the thoughts, feelings, and physical sensations that showed up when she thought of each value.

She realized one of the reasons for her resistance to completing the "Values Assessment" exercise. *For 40 years, she had been using her mother's values to direct her life.* By seeing her inner values, Elise was able to become more selective about the clients she accepted and whom she spent her time with. After 18 months of aligning all decisions around her values, Elise was feeling very successful. She eliminated her debt, increased her profits by 45%, and was energized by her business. In addition, Elise let go of friendships that were not in alignment with her inner values. For the first time, she had a relationship with a man based on integrity, adventure, and deep caring.

#### ---- Exercise ----

### Values Assessment

*Identify Your Top Five Values*

Read the following condensed list of values. Circle five words that ring true as a VALUE for you.

You are looking for a VALUE, a personal compass – not a "want," "should" or something external. *A VALUE gives your life purpose and acts as a rudder to your personal voyage.* Be willing to look at the list and try on each of the words. Write down a word that resonates with you – even if you don't think it could possibly be a value. There is significance in that resonance; you may have discovered a hidden value.

| | | |
|---|---|---|
| Achievement | Happiness | Prosperity |
| Adventure | Helping Others | Respect |
| Affection | High Standards | Satisfaction |
| Ambition | Honesty | Security |
| Authenticity | Honor | Self-expression |
| Authority | Humor | Self-reliance |
| Autonomy | Imagination | Sincerity |
| Belonging | Independence | Spirituality |
| Challenge | Integrity | Stability |
| Clarity | Joy | Status |
| Connections | Leadership | Success |
| Control | Leisure | Taking risks |
| Cooperation | Love | Tradition |
| Exercise | Loyalty | Tranquility |
| Fame | Order | Travel |

| Family | Outdoor Life | Trust |
| Freedom | Patience | Truthfulness |
| Friendship | Power | Wealth |
| Fun | | Well-being |

*Prioritize Your Top Five Values*

Fill in the chart following these steps; leave shaded squares blank. (Note: Refer to the sample chart provided in the "Needs Assessment" exercise.)

1. In the TOP ROW of boxes, write your five values in any order.
2. In the FAR LEFT COLUMN, write your five values in the same order as the top row.
3. Compare the value in the TOP BOX OF THE LEFT COLUMN with the FIRST BOX OF THE TOP ROW. Which one do you need most? *If one value seems to fit under the umbrella of another, choose the one that is larger.* Following across and down on the grid, write down the most important of the two values in the first available open square.
4. Continue this process until you've filled in all the open squares.
5. Count how many times you wrote each value in the grid. On the lines underneath the grid, write down the value with the number next to it. (Note: When the numbers are added together, the total of the numbers should be 10.)

**Your Values Assessment Chart**

| | | | | |
|---|---|---|---|---|
| | | | | |
| | | | | |

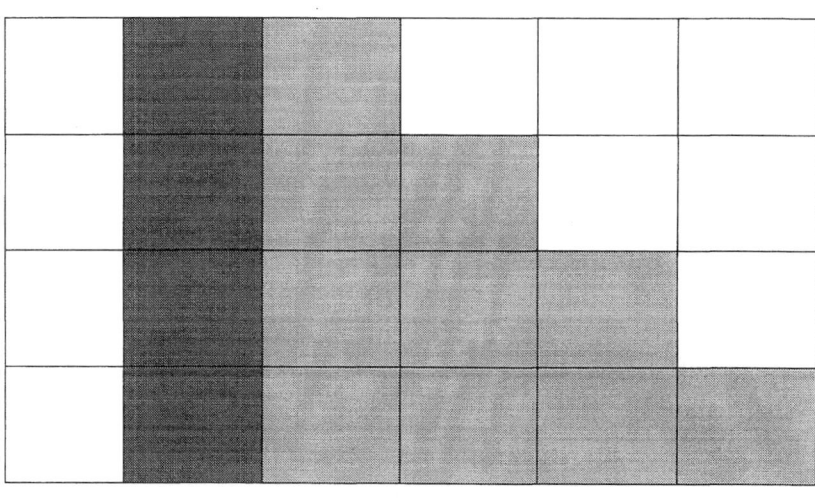

---- **Exercise** ----

**Fine-Tuning Your Inner Value Resonance**

In this exercise, you will explore what each value means to you. In your journal, notebook or computer file, write your answers to the following questions. Think about how each value resonates with you.

1.    Beginning with your top value, write your own personal definition for this word. Then write a description of the thoughts, feelings, and physical reactions you have when you think about the word.

2.    Now write a definition and description for each of your remaining four values.

3.    Review your career. Is the work you are doing in alignment with these values?

4.    Review your relationships. Review how you spend your free time. Is this time spent in alignment with your values?

5.    What is the most important thing for you to do in your life right now?

6.    What area of your life has the biggest disconnection between your values and how you are living?

7.    What are the three most important changes you will need to make to effectively use your inner values to set your course and steer your path?

--------

## PART 3

## Powerful questions to navigate by

> "The words that enlighten the soul are more precious than jewels." ~ Hazratinayat Kahn

Questions are the power source for our thoughts. A powerful question stops you in your tracks. A powerful question makes you reflect and ponder. A powerful question can make you uncomfortable and squirm. A powerful question opens up many possibilities for you to explore. Using powerful questions to tap into your inner compass will build momentum and keep you on course.

On the following pages, I have included many powerful questions arranged by life and business situations. Read the questions. In your journal, notebook or computer file, write down your answers to the questions that intrigue you. If you are resisting or reacting emotionally to any question, take a closer look at it. Answer the question and explore what is behind the resistance or emotional charge.

Some will be excellent questions to ask your friends, colleagues, employees and coworkers. Do not be attached to the answers, just see where the questions take you.

#### ---- Exercise ----
### Questions for Your Senses

If you were to describe yourself as a fruit, what fruit would you be? Why? What senses would you use to describe the fruit?

What would you choose as your theme song?

Would you choose a different theme song for your work and personal lives?

How would you decorate or design your office if you had the chance and the choice?

If you had one hour today with absolutely nothing to do, what would you do?

If time stood still for one hour each day, what would you do during that hour? Would your activity for that hour vary by the day of the week or the season?

If you didn't hold back in your life, what would you be doing?

If you could trust that your family would be fine, what would you do with the rest of your life?

If you knew that you are beautiful just as you are, what would change for you?

When was the last time you felt passionate about your work?

What kind of work are you really passionate about?

What is the most difficult time of day to receive criticism? What do your senses tell you at this time of day? Is there a fragrance, thought or sound that comes to mind?

If you had connections and could be in any movie you chose, what movie would it be and what part would you play?

How do you reward yourself for getting a large project or unpleasant task done?

## Self-Discovery Questions

If you were to describe yourself as a Disney character, who would you be? Why?

If you could meet one historical figure, who would it be?

When the phone and the doorbell ring at the same time, which do you answer first?

Who was one of your childhood heroes?

What was the last book you read cover to cover?

What is one thing you have always meant to do?

If you could travel anywhere in the world, where would you go?

Which would be more difficult for you: training to run a five-minute mile or learning to play violin?

If you wake up tomorrow and things are just the way you want, what would be different about your life?

What do you "really" want?

What questions should you be asking yourself?

What is life asking you to do differently?

What goal are you ready to achieve?

If your company were an animal, what kind would it be?

If you knew that you are vital to your organization's success, how would you approach your work?

If things could be exactly right for you in the following situation
_____, how would they have to change?

If a doctor told you that your life depends on your changing the
way you live, what would you do first for yourself?

What's holding you back the most?

What is your philosophy on life?

What one thing should you take the initiative to start?

### Self-Discovery Questions (Work Related)

If you could break all the rules, which one would you start with?

If you could be trained in one new skill, what would it be?

Are you ever difficult to work with?  When and how are you
difficult?

If you were to become the CEO at your workplace, what
problem would you solve first?  How would you do it?

What are the most unproductive tasks you are responsible for?

If you trusted that your excellence would not put others in your
shadow, what would your one-year goals be?

What do you see yourself doing five years from now?

How do you think outsiders view your company?  What areas
need more improvement?  What can you do to change or
capitalize on that perception?

What parts of your job can you control?  Are you consciously
making choices about what you can control or are you
unconscious?

If you knew that you are as intelligent as your bosses, how
would you present yourself to them?

What are you wasting your time with?

What is the best career decision you've ever made? While making the decision, what messages where you getting from your senses? Describe the messages from all your six senses.

What do you love about your job?

What activities can you spend less time on and still obtain acceptable results?

Who was the best boss you've ever had? What do you look for in a great boss?

Who was the worst boss you have ever had? What gift did you get from having that experience?

If you were in a senior management position – and money was no object – what benefit or perk would you make available to your employees? Why?

If you could have any job at your current company, which would you choose? What strengths do you have that would make you good at this new job?

Would you rather receive cash, a gift certificate or public recognition as a work gift? Why?

What is the worst career decision you've ever made?

What activities can you delegate?

What is your most productive time of day? What are you usually doing at this time?

Think of a business leader you respect or admire. What do you look for in someone you respect and admire?

--------

By answering these powerful questions, you'll discover many new things. *What you want more of in your life. What you are ready to let go of.* You may even discover things that are very important to you, but you never given yourself permission or time to consider.

Read over the answers and pick out any patterns. Look for areas in your work and life where resistance is holding you back. What would you do if you remembered that you have a choice about everything in your life?

Step 4 will give you simple practices you can use to be totally at choice. You will find strategies for getting off the "should express". You will also discover how to make choices consciously that build on your strengths and move you into action to create what is really important to you.

Turn the page and start making choices... getting focused... setting goals...and thinking strategically about creating the *soul of success* in your life.

# STEP 4

## Creating from Choice

*"Far better it is to dare mighty things,*
*to win glorious triumphs, even though checkered by failure,*
*than to rank with those poor spirits who neither enjoy much*
*nor suffer much, because they live in the gray twilight that*
*knows no victory nor defeat."*
*~ Theodore Roosevelt*

You've worked hard and started to tap into what's important for you by reading and completing the exercises in Steps 1-3. I hope you have gained many insights, dropped some Limiting Beliefs, and really begun to discover an in-depth answer to the following question:

*"What do I really want my life and my career to do for me?"*

A key element to the *soul of success* is becoming totally at choice in everything you do. "I don't really have a choice" is a very common refrain when people feel stuck in a work or life situation that is unacceptable to them. You always have a choice. Usually, every situation offers many choices and possibilities. You just cannot see them because you are not used to looking.

Most of us have learned to do things based on advice or coercion from others. We want to avoid unpleasant or unwanted consequences. Often we do things to fill an unconscious need regardless of unhealthy consequences for us. We react to situations, stimulus, and learned behavior, forgetting that we have at least one choice, if not more... and we can be totally at choice in everything we do.

Conscious choice is the muscle we need to strengthen. When we do things for other reasons, we are making choices at each step in our journey. We are just not making them consciously. Our lives feel manipulated – swept away in the tide or at the mercy of other people's whims and actions.

*IF "NO" IS NOT AN OPTION, "YES" IS NOT A CHOICE.*

True choice is a skill rarely taught, but essential to a rich meaningful life. It takes time and awareness to develop. You will need to be vigilant as you strengthen this skill of being totally at choice. Others may be threatened by the idea and block your efforts to perfect the skill. Fear and lack of support holds these people back from being at choice. Not wanting to be left behind, they try to pull you back into reacting to consequences instead of moving forward from choice.

### Case Study: Awareness is the First Step to Being Totally At Choice

Terry was dissatisfied with his job. More than that, he really did not have a sense of his life having any meaning. Terry was certain that he didn't have a choice. Awareness of choice was a very difficult shift for Terry to make.

Avoiding consequences had always been his reason for doing things. For example, Terry thought that good grades meant you didn't get grounded. Paying your mortgage on time kept the bank from foreclosing. We go along to get along.

I asked Terry to be aware of why he did everything he did for a week. He made a list separated into two columns. The first column was labeled CONSEQUENCES; the second column was labeled CHOICE. At the end of the week, the CONSEQUENCES column had many more things listed. After talking about each activity on Terry's list, we noticed that an interesting pattern emerged in the CHOICE column.

In the CHOICE column, the following activities were listed: energy, meaning, and satisfaction. It also included creativity and strategies used on some of the projects. The CONSEQUENCES column included working on projects or meeting deadlines. This exercise gave Terry awareness of choice. With this awareness, he could approach his projects differently. Instead of just doing them in a prescribed way, he would look at a variety of ways to complete the projects.

Today, Terry applies a new approach based on his preferences: (1) thinking strategically; (2) getting projects accomplished in a timely manner; and (3) approaching projects more creatively. His new approach comes from CHOICE not from consequences. It gives him energy, a sense of satisfaction, and a professionally completed project that is much more fun to work on.

Terry built this awareness of choice by taking a fresh look at every one of his activities at work. The results were terrific. Terry streamlined procedures and instituted a program that put awareness of choice into the team dynamic. The VP of Terry's division noticed a big change in team dynamics, efficient use of systems, and workflow patterns. Six months later, Terry was promoted to Project Leader.

By using your values as a guide for making choices, you'll find it much easier to perfect the skill of being totally at choice. In Step 3, you completed a "Values Assessment" exercise. This exercise was a simple yet direct tool for guiding your choices with inner values.

Write your top five values from the "Values Assessment" exercise on a small Post-It® note or index card. Keep the card visible when you are making choices. It can help you align the choices with your values. You'll find it much easier and fulfilling to make decisions based on choice – guided by your inner compass – rather than by consequences.

Making choices based on what is really important to you and your life purpose reduces or totally removes conflict and struggle from the decision process.

## *Case Study: Combine Inner Values with Awareness of Choice*

Elise's alternative health practice brought her fulfillment and satisfaction. However, she wanted to generate more revenue from her business. She realized her business was successful on many levels, but the success was not whole. Elise was missing the *soul of success;* her business really was not supporting her and her vision for her life.

Through our coaching sessions, Elise was able to combine her awareness of choice with her inner values to create her success. She developed a strategic plan for business growth by using her top five values: integrity, freedom, creativity, nature, and passion.

I asked Elise to develop a set of criteria she could use to review business opportunities. The criteria were based on her values and what she wanted her business to do for her. These criteria incorporated her feelings, her vision for the business, and what she wanted the business to bring into her life.

As each opportunity presented itself, she used the criteria as a tool. This tool helped her gauge each opportunity's value to her business. *It allowed her to make value-centered decisions.* It enabled her to remove emotions from a decision and take a strategic approach, which was very helpful in stressful or very busy periods in her business cycle.

This tool allowed her to stay focused on the areas she was most passionate about. It also helped Elise feel confident she was not turning down valuable opportunities. Elise was able to keep focused, strategic and balanced while substantially boosting her profits.

---- **Exercise** ----

## Business Opportunity Review Worksheet

This worksheet will help you sort through opportunities that come your way. You can use it as a tool to decide if taking the opportunity will move you in the direction you really want to go.

Many times, we take an opportunity because we think it's good and we *shouldn't* pass it up. However, it really isn't the right direction for us to be moving in. Perhaps it isn't the best time to pursue it. Or modifications are needed to make it a win-win opportunity.

This tool will allow you greater clarity in making these decisions. You can use the criteria you have selected to measure each opportunity. Rather than making a decision as a reaction to the circumstances or based on being caught up in the moment, this worksheet enables you to step back and take an objective view. You will be able to assess each opportunity and determine if it will help you reach your goals.

List your top five inner values:

1.                              4.
2.                              5.
3.

For each of these inner values, answer the following question:
How will _____ (this opportunity) support my value
of _____?

You will find you list at least two criteria in answer to each question. Some of your criteria may be similar for different values. You will need to write five criteria on your Business Opportunity Review Worksheet.

Example

Question: *How will the opportunity of this <u>radio interview</u> support my value of <u>freedom</u>?*

Answer: *Promoting my book via radio gives me more <u>flexibility,</u> I can keep my life and business schedule <u>balanced</u> by not having to travel all the time but still <u>reach audiences</u> in other parts of the country.*

*The criteria pulled from this example are:*
I have flexibility of time and effort in my activities and schedule.
Balance with my work and life or my time in general. The return
I get from the opportunity will be greater than the amount of
effort I put into the opportunity.

## SAMPLE

## Business Opportunity Review Worksheet

Use the following chart as an example to fill out your Business
Opportunity Review Worksheet. Make sure you write a clear
definition of why each criterion is important to you.

| Criteria | Why This Criteria is Important | Opportunity | Rating 1-10 |
|---|---|---|---|
| Fun | This opportunity will be fun and will not feel like work. | | 9 |
| Effort / Reward | The reward will be in line with the amount of effort. | | 2 |
| Flexibility | This opportunity gives me flexibility and choices. | | 6 |
| Balance | This opportunity allows me to stay balanced in work/life | | 6 |

You can make your own master of this worksheet. Select
criteria that are important to you and leave the rating column
blank. When a new opportunity arises, print off a new
worksheet. Think about the opportunity using your values to
keep you focused and allow you to be completely at choice
about the opportunity.

Set a minimum score you require the opportunity to rate for you
to consider acting on it. If the opportunity does not meet your
rating standard but you have a good feeling about it, see what
you can change in the opportunity to make it pull a better rating
on the worksheet.

--------

## PART 1

### Wisdom's Voice: Your inspiration

*"The aim of life is to live, and to live means to be aware,*
*joyously, drunkenly, serenely, divinely aware."*
~ Henry Miller

Have you ever heard a voice in your head tell you something that is about to happen? Have you ever heard a voice whisper a great idea into your mind? Have you ever picked up a very strong emotional or intuitive hit to act on a particular situation?

These situations are Wisdom's Voice speaking to you. What was your reaction? Did you listen? Did you ignore it? Did you discount the voice as something you made up? Part of honing and flexing your muscle of being totally at choice is using all of the helpful tools and gifts innately available to you. Two of these gifts are your INTUITION and ABILITY TO FOCUS.

These two gifts are integral to making concious choices in your life. What happens when we don't rely on our initution and focus? Confusion, struggle, and the sense of being overwhelmed play a large role in our daily activites.

#### ---- Exercise ----

#### Building the Skill of Power Focus

The exercise is great to help you relax and relieve tension. It gets you in the practice of POWER FOCUSING.

Find a quiet place you can sit without interuptions or the phone ringing for 15 minutes. If you can sit in nature while doing this exercise, the results will be even better. Sit in your yard, at the beach, by a stream or in a park. You will need blank sheets of paper, your favorite pen, and a sharp pencil.

1.  Start with the following breathing technique:
    *Sit in a comfortable position with the soles of your feet*
    *flat on the ground. Tense the muscles in your toes and*
    *feet. Really scrunch and tighten the muscles. Hold it*

*for a count of five and release all tension in that area. Tense your ankles and calves. Repeat technique of scruntching and tightning for a count of five... and then release the tension.*

*Now focus on tensing your knees and thighs, and repeat the same technique of tightning, holding, and releasing tension. Continue doing this for each region of our body as you move towards your head. Tense your backside and your lower back. Tense your stomach and upper back. Tense your shoulders and arms all the way to your fingers. Finish by tensing your neck and your brow. Then release all of the tension.*

2. Write down a brief discription of something you want to create or change in your life. Make the statement positive and specific.

   Examples of descriptions you want to focus on:
   Have fun and balance in my daily activites
   Strengthen my muscles and aerobic endurance

   "Lose weight" is not specific enough and is really a negative statement. "Not be stressed out" is vague and focused on what you don't want.

3. Put your paper, pen or pencil on the ground next to you. Sit up straight in a comfortable position with the soles of your feet flat on the ground. Continue with the following breathe focusing technique

   *Take a long, slow cleansing breath in through your nose and out through your mouth. Take another deep cleansing breath.*

   *Close your eyes and take another deep cleansing breath. As you finish exhaling this breath, bring the description you want to focus on into your mind.*

   *Just breath slowly and deeply, while focusing on the description. See in your mind what the words look like. Hold your focus on the discription and just notice*

*everything that comes to you. Notice any fragrance that comes to mind. Notice any sounds or quotes that come to mind. Notice any phsical sensations you experience while focusing on the description.*

*Take a long slow, deep breath, and repeat the description silently to yourself three times. Hold your focus on the description for several more slow, deep breaths.* Now slowly open your eyes.

4. Write down everything your six senses brought to you about the discription you were focusing on:
   - What fragrances came to you?
   - What sounds or quotes came to you?
   - Did you hear music or get the sense of a song?
   - What were you feeling?
   - What physical sensations did you notice?

5. Check in with your heart what came to you from the heart. Don't edit. There are no wrong or right answers. It's all about tapping into your wisdom's voice and focusing on what you want. Take a few more minutes to write down any last thoughts about this exercise. Set down your pieces of paper, and take three deep cleansing breaths.

6. Pick up a blank sheet of paper. While you were doing this exercise an image will have come into your mind. Some people will see it clearly like a picture, some will get a "sense" of a picture, and some will use language to create the image.

   Draw a picture that illustrates what came to your mind when concentrating on description of your focus. There's no need to be an artist. Just sketch what visual came to you. There may be several separate images. Don't edit. Draw anything that pops into your mind. Don't struggle with the drawing. Resist thinking you are just making up the image. Just put a pencil to the piece of paper and let all, images flow.

7. Using the description of your focus label your drawings and keep these papers in a file on your desk.

--------

By doing this exercise several times every week, you'll build up your Power Focus muscle. It helps you spend time getting centered and focusing all of your senses on what is important to you. Don't forget to save your sketches. Later in the book, I'll introduce other exercises that will provide greater insight, focus and detail into those sketches.

## Case Study: Power Focus Combined with Positive Thought Attracts Opportunities

Joni had made great progress in isolating and eliminating the negative talk from her inner critic. As a result of our coaching sessions, she was able to focus on making opportunities and fun flow into her life.

In the "Power Focus" exercise, Joni spent a lot of time working on the following description: *Bringing together talented people to help women balance life and work.* When she first wrote it, Joni had no idea what form the description would take. It was just a passion of hers – an idea that was not quite complete yet really resonated with her.

Joni used this description in four separate "Power Focus" exercises. She saved all of her writing and sketches. She was intrigued by some of the images and thoughts her senses were bringing to her.

During our next coaching call, Joni was excited yet puzzled. The night before, she had an intense dream about an event that incorporated the description from her "Power Focus" exercise. She was puzzled about the timing of the dream, because she hadn't thought about her "Power Focus" exercises for over a month. She had been extremely busy working on two events. Joni's thoughts had been totally occupied by her hectic schedule and glitches in venue arrangements, vendor contracts, etc.

The dream was very vivid. The event in the dream matched what Joni had put on paper. She was really excited to think about the possibilities of organizing such an event.

I asked Joni to write a letter to the event in the dream. I wanted her to write in a friendly, passionate voice about all of the things she wanted to bring to women with the event. I asked her to write as if the event were a close friend – and to describe all of the great things the two of them could do together.

During the weekend, Joni sat down to write her letter. Ideas flowed into her mind. As she thought of the event as a "friend," Joni imagined the two of them were having a discussion – and they were having this great brainstorming of possibilities.

As a result of writing the letter, Joni was able to really focus on the possibilities. She developed a strategic plan to make the event in her dream a reality.

Six months later, Joni organized and hosted a life fair for women. It incorporated alternative healers, coaches, personal trainers, spiritual healers, writers, and business people. The theme was bringing passion and balance back into women's lives. It was a great success. She had great fun organizing the event, while making many wonderful friendships and contacts that have benefited her life and her business.

### Being at Choice during Change and Transition

TRANSITION and CHANGE are two areas that bring up a lot of struggle for people. By tapping into your skill of Power Focus and being at choice, you can smooth out the waves and get to the other side. You'll be ready to move forward.

*Change is the only constant.* Many of my clients have discomfort with the topics of change and transition. Often, they feel bowled over by the events that bring about change. They see change as something that is *happening to them* – leaving them with no control and no choice.

By shifting our perspective and attitude about change, we can remove the struggle from new situations and transitions. *We always have a choice in our perspective and attitude.* We do not have to initiate change or transition to be in a position to choose our actions, reactions, and interactions during the process. It really requires you to choose your path rather than simply react to situations or events.

## ---- Exercise ----

### Your Letter for Letting Go and Creating an Ending

This exercise is perfect if you're experiencing any of the following situations:

- Transitioning from a business you own to a new business venture
- Transitioning from one job to another
- Transitioning from a relationship to being on your own
- Letting go of anger towards a boss or colleague
- Letting go of anger towards a parent
- Letting go of a child leaving home for college or life

NOTE: If you feel stuck or really overwhelmed by your situation, it will be helpful to do the "Power Focus" exercise first.

I find that typing this exercise into a computer file is the best approach for letting your thoughts flow. However, you can use whatever method is most comfortable for you – writing on special stationary, in your journal or notebook, etc.

Following are the steps to writing your letter:

1.    Get very clear about whom or what you are writing to. It can be a person, company or situation. Just make it clear in your mind that you are writing directly to that entity.

2.    Close your eyes and take some deep cleansing breaths. Get yourself centered without distraction before you begin.

3.    Hold a clear intent in your mind that you will let your thoughts and words flow, tapping into Wisdom's Voice. Do not edit as you write.

4.    Begin with "Dear..." Write with passion from your heart.

Possible points to cover in your letter include:

- *You taught me...*
- *I have learned so much about myself because of you...*
- *I am dissatisfied with you because...*
- *I know it's time to move on...*
- *I am ready to say goodbye because...*
- *During this time...*
- *I thank you for...*
- *Our many struggles and arguments taught me...*
- *What I will miss...*
- *What I won't miss...*
- *Our time together has opened up so many possibilities...*
- *It has been difficult, but I would not change a thing because...*
- *The greatest gift I brought to you...*
- *These are the strengths I take away...*

The power of this simple exercise will surprise you. It will set the stage for you to really move forward with your transition. By creating an ending, you will strengthen your new beginning.

--------

## PART 2

### The realm of all possibilities

*"Nothing can stop the person with the right mental attitude from achieving their goal; nothing on earth can help the person with the wrong mental attitude."* ~ *Thomas Jefferson*

Strategic thinking and envisioning what you want in your life is the next step in realizing real choice and clear direction. When was the last time you stopped and thought objectively about your life? We get so busy with the fast pace of our lives and trying just to keep up. It's difficult to take a step back and gain some perspective on what is actually important.

#### ---- Exercise ----

#### An Eagle's Perspective of Your Life

Pick up a small notebook you can easily carry everywhere.

You are going to get a different view; you will be taking notes of thoughts, impressions and ideas that come to you.

You'll need to keep the little notebook handy to write things down in the moment. Otherwise, you may not remember them. For the next five days, I want you to look at your life – all of it – from an eagle's perspective. You are going to consciously lift yourself out from your movie and take notes on what you see.

*Follow these steps for your daily notebook:*

1. **As you begin each day, answer these questions:**

   - How does your body feel when you wake up? Any aches or pains?

   - What is your energy level? Are you well rested or tired?

   - What is your attitude as you think about your work today?

   - What tone do you have in your voice when you greet the first person you see?

2. **While traveling to work, answer these questions:**

   - What interaction do you have with people as you travel to work?

   - What is the tone of the thoughts running through your head? Worried, positive, overwhelmed, swirling, etc?

   - As you walk into work, how would you rate your satisfaction with your job on a scale of 1-10 (10 being the best)?

3. **While taking time for lunch, answer these questions:**

   - How much time do you have for lunch today?

   - Is it a working lunch or are you having a fun casual lunch?

   - Check in with your body: How are you feeling?

What are you feeling?

- Look around as you walk back into your workplace. What is your impression of the mood of the people there?

- What are the first thoughts that enter your mind when get you back to work? Are you concentrating on a task...can't wait to leave...excited by the work you are doing...swirling and unfocused...?

4.   **When leaving work, answer these questions:**

- What are you feeling right now?

- As you walk out the door, how would you rate your satisfaction with your job on a scale of 1-10 (10 being the best)?

- What is your attitude as you think about tomorrow?

- What are you going to do just for you right now?

5.   **Before sleeping at night, answer these questions to complete your daily notebook:**

- How would you rate your energy level right now on a scale of 1-10 (10 being the highest)?

- Write at least four pages *(the pages are small, so no complaining here)* answering the following question: WHAT IS THE TRUTH ABOUT WHAT I DO FOR A LIVING?

   There is no wrong or right answer to this question. You are just exploring. Look at the fourth page of your writing on this question; this is where you will gain some real insights.

--------

### Case Study: Awareness is Key to Opening Up Possibilities

Sarah was really tired of the grind at work. More than three nights every week, she found herself working late. Every quarter, she would take on a couple of extra projects.

The "should express" was Sarah's motivation for taking on all of this extra work: *"I should stay late and finish a few more things; it will help me get ahead tomorrow."* *"I should take on that women's network project, because I would be seen as a team player."* *"I am ready to make a change; I should take on this project, so I can have documentation of this skill in my file."*

Sarah enjoyed doing the "Eagle's Perspective" exercise. It helped her become focused and aware of exactly what was happening each day. As she took a bird's eye view of her life, Sarah felt a sense of relief and detachment.

She made notes of how she felt at different parts of the day, as well as what was coming up or just occurred that made an impact in how she was feeling. One thing that fascinated her was being able to remain detached during a heated conversation with a coworker that we'll call "Bob."

Several times every month, Bob made a point to get into charged conversations with Sarah or his other coworkers. For the first time, Sarah clearly saw Bob getting energy from this exchange. She noticed that as Bob geared up for these encounters, his body language changed – he seemed to have a sense of mission and intent as he walked into her office.

She realized these confrontations were all about Bob. As a result of this newfound understanding, Sarah's next conversation with Bob was much shorter. It seemed to fizzle out. Sarah was able to be in a space of detachment, in which she didn't engage the conversation or take it personally.

In addition to helping resolve her challenges with Bob, the "Eagle's Perspective" exercise gave Sarah a new perspective on what was important to her. She realized her attitude was more important than what she was doing. How she did things mattered more than what she was doing.

From an eagle's perspective, Sarah developed a strategic vision of what she wanted in her life. She looked at the larger picture of the company and her place in it. She spent a few weeks exploring the possibilities of a career shift within and outside of the company. By using the eagle's perspective and thinking with a strategic approach, Sarah was able to shift the following three things in her life:

1.   *She diminished the sense of being overwhelmed and stressed.*

2.   *She focused on building a bigger vision for her life.* Sarah put together one and three year plans.

3.   *She felt whole.* Sarah stopped being one way at home and another way at work. She acknowledged her strengths, her natural style, and showed up at work as herself for the first time.

#### ---- Exercise ----

### Letter to Your Ideal Job, Employee, Relationship, Etc.

Putting what you want into writing is a powerful way to bring things into your life. Be clear, specific and positive.

The last step in the process of writing things down and putting them out to the universe is letting go of the outcome. Release yourself from becoming attached to the outcome. Trust that what you ask for – or something better – will come into your life.

Following are the steps to writing your letter:

1.   Set a clear intention about writing this letter. Believe in the power it will have to bring what you want into your life.

2.   Write the letter in a special place. You can go to the beach, a beautiful spot by a stream, your favorite coffee shop, etc.

3.   Settle your thoughts and take some clearing breaths before you begin writing.

4.   Focus on what you really want to bring into your life. Write the letter in the first person present tense with

positive statements.

5.      Date the letter and place it in a safe place in your room
        or office.

-------

## Case Study: Asking for What You Want Sets Things in Motion

Cheryl was frustrated at being passed over for the Managing Director position. She had an excellent record and outperformed all of the other sales professionals. We talked about why she wanted the position...how it would have fit into her long-range career goals...and what effect it would have had on her personal life.

Cheryl played out the "what if" scenarios for the position. She thought about her vision for the next five years – and the position she would *really* like to have in the company.

Cheryl wrote a letter to her ideal position. In the letter, she described the challenges and rewards the position would bring her. She explored her growth as a person, detailing opportunities that would come into her life because of this ideal position. Then she dated the letter and agreed to set it a side for three months before reviewing it.

We coached around strengthening her communication and presentation skills. Cheryl had taken on two special projects that required her to stretch in her communication skills. These two projects gave Cheryl some great networking opportunities. As a result of this networking, Cheryl took on a third project working for the VP of corporate sales. This new project also stretched her strengths, but she was enjoying the challenge.

Three months later, Cheryl read the letter written to her ideal position. She was surprised the three special projects met most of the criteria she had laid out. She discovered building on her strengths and continuing to grow were more important to her than a specific job title.

Cheryl did the exercise again. Four months later,

she made a move to corporate sales. At the same time, she was positioning herself for a move into corporate communications for West Coast divisions.

## PART 3
## Integrity Goals: Intention, alignment and fulfillment

> *"The minute you choose to do what you really want to do it's a different kind of life."*
> ~ *Buckminster Fuller, Inventor & Philosopher*

- *Goals chosen from your values and integrity give you energy.* They reflect your passion, your drive, and the things that are really important to you.

- *Goals formed while riding on the "should express" drain your energy.* Usually, these goals are based on other people's expectations and what they think is good for you.

Some people don't ever set goals. Usually, they are tired of not reaching unrealistic goals. Or perhaps these people found no satisfaction reaching goals that came from *someone else's* expectations rather than based on their *own* integrity and values.

Not having goals to bring you where you want to go in your life is like a pilot flying from Los Angeles to New York with no directions, no working fuel gauges, and no time of arrival.

Goals give us a sense of direction. They provide a sense of progress and a rudder to steer our course. When they are set using your inner values and aligned with your integrity, your goals will give good direction and monitor the progress you achieve.

### Five Essential Criteria for Setting Integrity Goals

1. They must be based on your inner values and give you a sense of possibility and energy.

2. They must be expressed in clear, detailed,

measurable and positive statements.

3.    They must be written down. Written goals crystallize your intention and make stronger motivational tools. They build momentum and bring you success.

4.    They must be large enough to make you stretch yet realistically achievable.

5.    They must be performance goals not outcome goals. Basing your goals on personal achievement keeps you in control of the end result and satisfaction you achieve from them.

#### ---- Exercise ----
### *Effective Goal Setting*

The steps outlined below will help you set effective goals designed specifically for you. Combined with the "Five Essential Criteria for Setting Integrity Goals," the following steps will take you through the process of setting, measuring, reaching and redefining your goals.

**Step 1:    Take an eagle's view of what you want to happen in your life.**

List all of the things you would like to do in your life. These are your LIFE VISION GOALS-- the big picture goals they usually represent a feeling or sense of being.

*Example:*
*   *I want to have a successful relationship.*
*   *I want to have a rewarding career doing something that I am passionate about.*
*   *I want to travel to many different countries.*
*   *I want to develop a life-training program for high school kids.*
*   *I want to have financial independence.*
*   *I want to be loving and not judge people.*
*   *I want to raise a child.*
*   *I want to live in a comfortable home surrounded by nature.*

You can always add or change this list later. It is just a place that will help you start thinking of a bigger vision for your life. At this point in the goal setting process, you are not worried about details. You are looking at the possibilities. You are thinking about what interests you and what you want your life and career to do for you.

**Step 2:  Put your Life Vision Goals into a loose time frame.**

Look at the Life Vision Goals that you wrote in Step 1 of this exercise. What is the order and time frame for achieving them?

As you work towards your goals, you can change this time frame around. It's just a place to start. By putting your Life Vision Goals into a loose time frame, you'll find it easier start making them happen.

*Example:*
- *I want to travel to many different countries – IN MY EARLY FIFTIES.*
- *I want to have financial independence – IN MY MID FORTIES.*
- *I want to develop a life-training program for high school kids – IN MY MID THIRTIES.*
- *I want to live in a comfortable home surrounded by nature – IN MY MID TWENTIES.*
- *I want to have a rewarding career doing something I am passionate about – IN MY LATE TWENTIES.*
- *I want to raise a child – IN MY EARLY TWENTIES.*
- *I want to have a successful relationship – IN MY EARLY TWENTIES.*
- *I WANT TO BE LOVING AND NOT JUDGE PEOPLE – NOW.*

Before you move forward with Step 3, reorder and prioritize your goals by using the time frames. In the example above the client is 21 years of age. Therefore, she would prioritize her goals with a time frame that starts with the goal she wants to achieve NOW. The time frame ends with the goal she wants to achieve in her early fifties.

**Step 3:** **Begin with the end in mind.**

Now you need to create MID-RANGE GOALS from the time frame you created in Step 2. Mid-Range Goals are blocked into strategic time frames, structured in 7-year, 5-year and 3-year periods.

Start with the 7-year period. Write down your Mid Range Goals to accomplish in seven years. For example, one of your 7-year Mid Range Goals is to have a child. Create a list of the action steps you will need to put into place to successfully accomplish that Mid Range Goal.

*Example:*

MID-RANGE GOAL= *TO HAVE A CHILD*

7yr:
- *Build my savings account balance*
- *find a loving partner*

5 yr:
- *Build my self-confidence*
- *Get physically fit*

3 yr:
- *Strengthen my relationships*
- *Take time to do things now that will be more difficult with a child.*

**Step 4:** **Laser Focus Goals move you forward to your Mid-Range Goals.**

LASER FOCUS GOALS are blocked into a time frame of 1-year, 6-month, and 3-month periods.

Select a Mid-Range Goal and create a Laser Focus Goal. Write the goal in tiered format, with the Mid-Range Goal on the top. Follow with supporting goals. Then put your Laser Focus Goals underneath. Place the 1-year, 6 months, and 3 months goals below that.

*Example:*

### LIFE VISION GOAL:

*I want to live in a comfortable home surrounded by nature.*

### MID-RANGE GOAL:

*Move into my house and easily afford the payments*
**7 Year Goal-** *Learn good money management skills.*
**5 Year Goal-** *Create a savings plan for a down payment*
**3 Year Goal** *Build up my credit rating.*

### LASER FOCUS GOALS:

**1 Year Goal-**
*Research the real estate market and the schools.*
Create criteria for my ideal home or piece of land.
**6 Month Goal-**
*Weigh the merits of building vs. buying a home.*
**3 Month Goal-**
*Select an area I want to live in.*

**Step 5:** **Momentum Goals keep you moving forward and motivated.**
MOMENTUM GOALS are blocked into a time frame of weekly and daily goals. These goals are small in scope but strategic in nature. Look at your Laser Focus Goals. Choose one to work on. Underneath the 3-month goal, write your Momentum Goals starting with the weekly one and then the daily ones. Keep these goals small and easy to accomplish.

Example:

### LIFE VISION GOAL:

*I want to live in a comfortable home surrounded by nature.*

### MID-RANGE GOAL:

*Move into my house and easily afford the payments*
**7 Year Goal-** *Learn good money management skills*
**5 Year Goal-** *Create a savings plan for a down*

*payment.*
**3 Year Goal-** *Build up my credit rating.*

### *LASER FOCUS GOALS:*

**1 Year Goal-**
*Research the real estate market and the schools.*
*Create criteria for my ideal home or piece of land.*
**6 Month Goal-**
*Weigh the merits of building vs. buying a home.*
**3 Month Goal-**
*Select an area I want to live in.*

### *MOMENTUM GOALS:*

**Weekly Goal:**
Save 10% of my income.
Only use my credit card for purchases I can pay off as soon as I get the bill.
Read a book or take a course that will help me more easily achieve my Laser and Mid-Range Goals.

**Daily Goal:**
Keep a positive attitude about reaching my goal.
Eat a bag lunch or eat at home and put the money saved into a saving account.
Write in my journal about what is important in my life, my career, and what makes me happy.

**Step 6:**   **Celebrate each goal no matter how small.**

It is essential to celebrate each goal. Celebrate smaller goals by taking a minute to reflect on what you have accomplished. Celebrate larger goals by giving yourself a reward that matches the size, scope and importance of the completed goal.

*Example: After spending two hours writing my Life Vision Goals, I cooked myself a special meal and watched my favorite movie. Each time I complete a small goal. I make sure to think about what I have accomplished and how it will move me forward to my bigger goals. When I complete a large goal, I celebrate with friends or take a day off to have fun and enjoy my life and everything I am grateful for.*

**Step 7:** **Review, reevaluate, and restate as you move forward.**

We are constantly changing, growing and evolving along our life path. What you have learned and how you have grown will shape your Life Vision Goals. Set time aside once a year to REVIEW, REEVALUATE and RESTATE your Life Vision Goals. This yearly "3 R's" exercise will keep you on track with goals that are important and meaningful to you.

*Example:* *I make a ritual out of reviewing my Life Vision Goals once a year. I go to an inn or small cabin and plan what I want to keep moving forward with and what I want to change.*

--------

Setting goals in several areas of your life gives you a broad, balanced approach in creating success on your own terms. Examples of areas in your life for setting goals could include:

| Attitude | Education | Physical |
|----------|-----------|----------|
| Creative | Family | Public Service |
| Career | Financial | Spiritual |
| | Play | |

Remember the point of having goals is to serve you – not for you to be a slave to them. Setting integrity goals aligned with your inner values will bring you pleasure, satisfaction, and a sense of fulfillment. These goals are tools to create the *soul of success.*

## STEP 5

### Communicating the Complete Picture

*"A powerful agent is the right word.
Whenever we come upon one of those intensely
right words in a book or newspaper the resulting effect is
physical as well as spiritual, and electrically prompt."*
~ *Mark Twain*

Communication affects us internally and externally. Your words form 7% of your total communication, while your tone of voice is 38% and your gestures are 55%. Yet most people think communicating is one person saying something and having it reach another's ears.
*Are you good at communicating the complete picture?*

Following are Seven Essential Skills to Communicating the Complete Picture:

1.      Being Laser
*When you are speaking, do you keep your ideas and words focused and laser-like? Or do you ramble, creating a word maze that people get lost in?*

2.      Active Listening
*When you're in a conversation, are you really listening? Or are you thinking of what you are going to say when the other person stops talking?*

3.      Removing Judgment
*When you are communicating, are you listening and speaking from an open perspective or are you judging? Does the attachment you hold to your point of view get in the way of exploring another perspective?*

4.      Removing Self-Talk
*What is your self-talk like? Is it positive and supportive or negative and limiting? How does the tape of the inner critic affect your communication with yourself and others?*

5.      Awareness of Natural Style
*Everyone has a natural style of communicating. These styles and tendencies affect your behavior, your approach to a subject, and even your ability to listen. What is your natural style? How does it improve or hamper your effective communications?*

6.      Interest / Intent
*How does your interest in the outcome affect your communication style? Do you find it difficult to release your attachment to the outcome and work for a win-win position?*

7.      Powerful Questions
*Do you use questions as a powerful tool in communicating the complete picture? When you ask a question, are you looking for an answer that will move the communication forward? Or are you just looking for a confirmation of your point of view?*

As you work through the exercises in Step 5, you will discover how active listening improves your communication skills. You will find new depth and richness in your connections and conversations with people. You will also see a profound difference in how people communicate with you.

### Case Study: Sometimes We Say One Thing and People Hear Another

Robyn was responsible for supervising a 10-member team on a special project. It was off to a very slow start. As the project continued, Robyn found that each day was more frustrating than the last.

She was particularly frustrated because people were not taking any initiative to solve problems on their own. Robyn delegated tasks to the team members. However, she found herself spending more time answering the team members' questions about their responsibilities then if she had done the job herself. By doing exercises related to styles and strategies for communicating the complete picture, Robyn discovered she was being unclear and sending mixed signals.

The first step to resolving her challenges was communicating clearly with HERSELF. Robin needed to eliminate or change her self-talk, so it reflected the job she wanted to accomplish and the strengths she brought to the task. She also needed to get clear on what her expectations were for each team member and the completed project.

Robyn developed a checklist for team members. When accepting new tasks, they simply took a few minutes to review the checklist. The team members could then see if they needed to ask Robyn for additional information *before* they began working on their new responsibilities.

Robyn significantly improved the effectiveness of her communications by taking two approaches: (1) clearly laying out her expectations, and (2) providing resources for people to find the answers on their own. As a result, she removed the energy drain of delegating tasks and completed the project on time.

#### ---- Exercise ----

#### Look for the Picture in Every Communication

In this exercise, you will pay attention to every nuance of communication you have with yourself and everyone else.

Starting tomorrow, you will look for the complete picture in every communication. When you are communicating, be clear and remember to use all of your six senses: sight, sound, smell, touch, taste, and intuition. When you combine your six senses into the art and technology of communicating, you achieve what I call HEART TUNING. It helps you communicate the complete picture with whomever you are interacting with.

1.    Starting tomorrow, <u>use the following communication strategies</u> throughout the day:

    ***Things for you to do:***

    - Look people in the eye.
    - Really listen from the heart.
    - Use a clear, concise approach to get your message across. (Example: If you want to get together with someone, ask directly rather than hedging and rambling. Direct Approach: *I am going to have lunch in the park today would you like to join me.* Rambling & Hedging: *It's a nice day and it's kind of stuffy in the office. I was thinking of maybe going out to have lunch in the park. What are you doing for lunch maybe you would like to come too? If not it's okay I understand.*
    - Match tone and body language. (Example: If you tell someone how happy you are for them, don't speak in a low, tired tone of voice with slumped shoulders.)
    - Suspend your point of view.
    - Ask open-ended questions.
    - Pay attention to your natural style of communicating.

    These communication strategies are integral to the Seven Essential Skills to Communicating the Complete Picture.

    1. Being Laser
    2. Active Listening
    3. Removing Judgment
    4. Removing Self-Talk
    5. Awareness of Natural Style
    6. Interest / Intent
    7. Powerful Questions

In addition to the communication strategies, use the following observational strategies throughout the day. Keep in mind the "Seven Essential Skills to Communicating the Big Picture" to improve your connections with people.

***Things to observe about others:***

* Do they make eye contact with you?
* Are they listening?  Do you feel heard?
* Are they easy to understand?  Do they get to the point?
* Does their body language, expression, and tone of voice match what they are saying?
* Are they hearing your point of view?
* What kind of questions are they asking you?  Do you think they are genuinely interested in the answer?
* What qualities can you list about their natural style?

2. After each conversation, ask yourself the following questions and jot down a few notes about how you communicated in the conversation:

   * Did you remember to really listen?
   * Where you concise and laser like?
   * Did you have a judgment about the communication?
   * Did you ask powerful questions?

3. Write a paragraph about what you think was communicated in every conversation you had during the day.  Make sure to include the conversations you had with yourself or the conversation your inner critic had with you.

4. Take a few deep breaths.  Get centered and review all the times today you thought you were really communicating clearly.  On a scale of 1- 10 (10 being the best), how would you rate your communication skills and your ability to communicate the complete picture?

--------

## PART 1

### Active listening: The best communication tool

*"To listen well is as powerful a means of communication and influence as to talk well."* ~ *Chief Justice John Marshall*

Look at the word LISTEN and you will find an anagram for how to practice active listening: SILENT.

Step 4 focused on creating from choice. Remembering the muscle of choice and learning to flex and strengthen it through active listening is vital to communicating the complete picture. Having this muscle well defined will allow you to create what you want in your life, tapping into your personal power and increasing your opportunities and choices.

When we really listen to what is being said and left unsaid, we deepen our ability to communicate. Listening involves more than your ears picking up sound. *It involves all six senses.*

### Case Study: Listening is a Skill That Takes Practice

Julie thought she was a great listener. She always made time to listen to friends and colleagues; people felt comfortable sharing their thoughts, feelings, exciting news, struggles. Working with the "Seven Essential Skills for Communicating the Complete Picture," Julie realized active listening took a lot of practice.

Julie became aware of her communication style and skills. Then she worked to improve them. She discovered the skill that helped her most was *turning off her self-talk while communicating with others.* It removed distractions so she could listen intently. In addition, it eliminated the habit of thinking about what she was going to say when the other person stopped talking.

Working with the "Seven Essential Skills of Communicating the Complete Picture" dramatically improved Julie's communications. She felt much more organized and in control of her time. What she wanted to communicate and what the other person heard were finally matching up. There was less confusion working on projects and delegating became much more efficient, because Julie improved her ability to give directions, expectations, and an explanation of desired results was improved.

#### ---- Exercise ----
### Remove "I" or "Me" from Your Conversations

Communicating effectively is possible when you listen deeply. In order to use active listening, you need to be aware of all your senses and give your attention to the other person. The quickest way to do that is to remove the word "I" or "Me" from your conversations. Why? Because the communication then becomes all about the other person!

*This exercise is tough, so start out slowly.*

**Day #1:** Make a conscious note every time you use the word "I" or "Me" in a conversation with someone. Just notice when you say it.

**Day #2:** Write down each time you use the word "I" or "Me" in a conversation with someone. Keep a running tally.

**Day #3:** During ONE conversation today, choose to keep the focus on the other person every time you are about to use "I" or "Me" (Example: Someone is relating a story about a dinner experience, instead of just hearing what they are saying really listen to them. Instead of thinking of what you are going to say when they stop talking give them your complete attention. Instead of saying "I had a situation like that happen to me" or "I know what you mean, every time I go out those things always happen to me..." Focus on what they are telling you there feelings and experiences were, otherwise you move the conversation to focus on you! The other person doesn't feel heard. In fact, they are probably getting tired of you always directing the conversation to focus on you.)

**Day #4:** During TWO conversations today, choose a different word every time you are about to use "I" or "Me."

**Day #5:** Don't use the word "I" or "Me" the whole day.

*Wrap up this exercise as follows:*

**Wrap-Up:** At the end of Day #5, take 30 minutes to write down your thoughts about this exercise:

- Was it easy or hard?

- Where you surprised how many times you used the word "I" or "Me" in a conversation with someone?

- How did the quality of your conversations and your ability to listen change after removing the word "I" or "Me" from your conversations?

--------

### Case Study: It's Hard to Remove "You" as the Focus

Lauren was surprised by the difficulty of the "Remove Me Or I from Your Conservation" exercise. She considered herself a good listener – someone who was always open to the other person's point of view. On Day #2 of the exercise, Lauren discovered that she used the words "I" or "Me" over 75 times in her conversations.

Day #3 was exhausting for Lauren. She was determined to listen more intently and focus on the other person. However, she found that substituting a different word for "I" or "Me" made conversations seem stilted and confusing. She called me in the middle of the day for some spot coaching.

I suggested she change her perspective rather than try to change the words as they were coming out of her mouth. I asked her to have the intention to just listen and not add her experiences or opinion; which would greatly reduce the number of times the words "I" or "me" would come to mind.

I asked her what small shift would she need to make to have the conversation flow and not use the words "I" or "Me." Lauren replied, "I guess if I slowed down and listened without wanting to add to the conversation or fix something."

Having the awareness of what she needed to do to strengthen her communication was the first step to communicating the complete picture and actively listening. For Lauren, it was a long and difficult process to make the shift from hearing people to listening and communicating the complete picture. It took several weeks before Lauren found herself regularly using active listening and communicating effectively.

Old habits are hard to break. It took a lot of conscious effort for Lauren to strengthen her active listening skills. We coached around her communication and presentation skills. In addition, we removed some old scripts of self-talk from her patterns of thinking.

Three months later, active listening was much easier for Lauren. She still worked at the exercise of removing "I" or "Me" from her conversations to keep the focus on the other person. However, her communication muscles were growing along with her skill for being at choice.

The exercise of removing "I" or "Me" really improved Lauren's communication skills. Her colleagues commented on the change in Lauren, although they couldn't quite put their finger on what it was. They said Lauren seemed more relaxed and caring. Her boss noticed the changes, too. He asked Lauren to take a role implementing strategies for improving communication in the office.

### Removing judgment will help you actively listen

Just like a strong blustery wind can make things sound muffled or distort the direction a sound is coming from, judgment muffles what people are trying to communicate.

Sometimes this happens because our need to be heard, to be right, is so strong it interferes with our skill of communicating. Sometimes our ego needs to be in control of the conversation, at the center of attention, which gets in the way of understanding people

If these subtle forces are in the conversation, they create a wind that keeps the communication from being clear.

The wind also muffles the conversation when it comes from the judgment of low self-esteem; the voice of the inner critic is loud and drowns out our Wisdom's Voice. A good example is when you feel the need to disappear in a conversation, making the other person right, so you aren't noticed.

There isn't clear communication or a complete picture when this happens. It's hard to do your work or live your life when you are not willing to show up.

In order to communicate without judgment, you need to come from a new perspective.

There are no sides. Opinions are equal. And "it" just is. Exploring communication without judgment gives you common ground and a place to create understanding. Essentially, it enables you to move forward.

#### ---- Exercise ----

### Stand in Someone's Perspective

When doing this exercise, you must come from a place of integrity. You don't want to pretend or say something you don't believe. You want to look for an opportunity to be open to a different perspective.

*Over the next five days, you will hold a specific intent during at least five conversations:*

**1st Intent:**     During a conversation, tell someone you think he or she is really right about something.

**2nd Intent:**     During a conversation, tell someone that you completely understand his or her point of view.

*After the conversations, write down what you experienced during both the 1st and 2nd intents.*

•     Did you notice any changes in the communication between you and the other person?

•     How did it affect the outcome of your conversation?

•     Did the person change his or her style of communicating?

--------

The "Stand in Someone's Perspective" exercise is valuable because it makes us listen more intently. It makes us step away from a preconceived outcome and look for other possibilities.

Actively looking for an opportunity to acknowledge someone's opinion- to tell them we completely understand their point of view- makes it easier to listen more intently and helps the other person really feel heard. We begin to communicate the complete picture. We don't come to the conversation with half the picture already filled in. We stand in the moment and really communicate with someone else.

Really listening to someone is one of the greatest compliments and gifts you can give to them. In the next exercise, you will practice deepening that listening by shifting to listening with your heart.

---- **Exercise** ----

## Shifting the Place You Listen From

Listening with your heart instead of your head gives you a different perspective. It gets you out of judgment and shuts down the inner critic. You clear the space between your ears to be in tune with the other person you are communicating with. You stand in the present moment, as you actively and intently listen to the individual.

Over the next three days, you'll practice listening from the heart. Keep the other listening exercises in mind and just be totally present in your interactions.

You'll notice that this exercise doesn't include many steps, because it is about "being" rather than "doing."

**Action #1:**    Practice listening from your heart rather than your head. You can do this by silencing the chatter in your own mind. Don't analyze what is being said just listen. Pay attention to the emotional response in your body and the tone, and emotions of the other person.

**Action #2:**    Pay attention to what you hear when you listen with your heart.

**Action #3:**    In your journal, notebook or computer file, describe your observations as you listened with your heart:

- How did it change how you listened?

- How did it change how the other individual spoke?

- How did it increase your understanding?

--------

Go back to your "Little Gems" book from Step 2. This earlier exercise also focused on listening from your heart. By becoming aware of people's positive communication to you – both verbally and non-verbally – you were listening from your heart. You stopped the inner critic that played the tape to reinforce your limiting beliefs. You became more aware of the nuance of communication between people. You acknowledged and shared the "Little Gems" that people gave you throughout the day.

The following exercise will help you fine-tune your skill of listening from the heart.

#### ---- Exercise ----
#### Listen for Values and Strengths

In Step 3, you explored your inner compass and inner values. You looked at how you could create what you wanted in your life more successfully by using your inner values as a compass to set your course.

This exercise will help you become aware of other people's values and strengths through active listening. Developing the skill to identify someone else's inner values and strengths will improve your relationships and connections with people. It will prove particularly valuable in work settings when hiring people or selecting them for projects and management teams.

**Action #1:** Listen for values and strengths with everyone you come into contact with. Weave what you have learned about your listeners into the conversation.

**Action #2:** Practice the skill of reflecting back what you heard to each person you listen to. How does it change how you listen and what you hear?

**Action #3:** Write down your observations from the Actions #1 and #2:

- How did these steps raise the level of communication?

- What have you learned about the other persons in your conversations by listening their inner values and strengths?

--------

Active listening will help you be more at choice. When you listen to the complete picture, you tap into your personal power. You remove judgment, misunderstanding, and miscommunications. You make choices from a clear strategic, perspective. Working both your conscious choice muscles from Step 4 and your communication muscles from Step 5 will bring you swiftly to the *Soul of Success*.

## PART 2

## Self-Talk: Recognize it for what it is

*"The quieter you become, the more you can hear."*
~ *Baba Ram Dass*

We communicate in many ways. Some is direct active communication; some is indirect and passive. It is important to remember that communicating is much more than one person talking and the other person hearing.

When we communicate the whole picture, we use all of our six senses.

- We make eye contact or read the other person's body language.

- We hear background noises or any non-verbal noises fom the other person, such as a sigh or shallow breaths.

- Our noses provide clues in communication, as well. We may smell a person's perfume or cologne – or even scents from the surrounding environment.

- Communcation produces tastes, too. They are usually subtle and may go unnoticed. However, these tastes are part of the communication. For example, your mouth could be dry from nervousness about speaking or about what is being said.

• Touch is present in the communication, even when we are not in direct contact with the person we are speaking with. It may come through as a shiver or sensation of being warm and relaxed. While speaking, you make a real connection when putting your hand on the other person's shoulder. Studies have shown that sales – even tips to a waiter – will be increased if there is simple contact between the individuals.

• Intuition is the sixth sense we use when communicating the complete picture. We may pick up on how someone is feelingfrom the energy they are putting out. We may sense joy or worry in the person. Or we might have a sense of knowing and make our decisions based on it.

Heart Tuning is the word that I use to describe the use of all six senses in our communication. Heart Tuning allows us to be aware of the many layers of communication that are going on simultaneously. Heart Tuning gives you a real edge in communicating because employing all of your senses allows you to listen to what is being said, what is left un-said, and the intent behind the words.

Heart Tuning is also a wonderful skill to help tune out and turn off the inner critic. The skill of Heart Tuning heightens your awareness and makes it easier for you to decern the nature of your inner dialogue. It sorts the conversation in your mind into the following two categories: inner critic tapes and *Wisdom's Voice*. Just as you would carry on a conversation with someone else, you can communicate with your inner critic or *Wisdom's Voice*.

This communication is usually one-sided; our inner critic talks and we listen. Or our Wisdom's Voice speaks to us and we brush it away as something we made up. Why does this happen? Why is it easier to believe the negative and brush away the positive? *It's human nature.* For some reason, the negative communications have a way of sticking to us much more easily than the positive comments.

I believe the modeling each one of us receives from parents, friends, and teachers when we were young also plays a role in whether the negative or the positive sticks to us more. For example:

- If you were raised in a family where your strengths were applauded and you were encouraged to reach for what you wanted, it will be easier for you to hear *wisdom's voice.*

- If judgment and scarcity were the model you grew up with, your inner critic will speak more loudly to you.

When we use all six senses to communicate and flex our Heart Tuning muscles, we shift to a neutral perspective and can effortlessly communicate the complete picture.

### ---- Exercise ----
### Observe Your Self-Talk

You can remove the power that your self-talk has over you by becoming aware of who is really talking. By becoming the observer of your self-talk, you begin to end your resistance to it. You change the influence it has on your decisions and on your style of communication.

When you have quieted the self-talk from the inner critics, you will notice two things. *First, you will hear your Wisdom's Voice very clearly. Secondly, you will have more energy.* You will notice what a constant drain tolerating all that negative self-talk has placed on you each day.

Over the next week, become the observer of your self-talk.

1.      On the first day, simply notice the voice. Recognize it
        as the separate entity it is. These are not your
        thoughts, feelings, beliefs or words. They belong to the
        inner critic.

2.      During the rest of the week, actively listen to the inner
        critic and answer these questions.

   • Who is talking?

   • What is the value of what is being said?

   • What are the limiting beliefs behind what is being
     said?

   • Is this a protection measure? Are you scared to
     take action so you let the inner critic give you all
     sorts of evidence why it would be better not to take
     action?

   • What are you afraid of seeing clearly?

   • What is the truth for you about what the inner critic
     is saying?

--------

Self-talk is the main reason why people are
unfulfilled and businesses fail. The constant drain and
flow of negative energy can wear down even the most
resilient person. It clouds our thoughts and creative
ideas, and changes our style of communication. As we
discussed in Step 4, you have an innate gift in your
*Wisdom's Voice.*

Clearing our self-talk and practicing the skill of Heart
Tuning is like tuning a radio. It cuts out the static. It lets
the music and words that will serve and guide you to the
*soul of success* come though crystal clear.

### Explore your natural style of communicating

In order to communicate the complete picture, it
is important to speak from a point of strength using your
natural style of behavior and communication.

You can pick up language cues, body posture cues, etc. Volume, tone, and intention are all cues for you to discover your own or someone else's natural style of communicating.

*Things to look for in identifying a natural style:*

- Do you (they) speak loudly or softly?

- Do you (they) speak quickly or very slowly?

- Do you (they) use a lot of hand gestures?

- Do you (they) have animated expressions or reserved expressions?

- Do you (they) use simple language or words that add depth and meaning to the conversation?

- Do you (they) use language that suggests confidence or uncertainty?

- Do you (they) set a tone with the rhythm and cadence of your voice?

- Do you (they) want short, quick answers or more detail and specifics?

- Do you (they) make up your mind quickly or need more time to consider?

- Do you (they) use communication to be inclusive and build consensus, be directive or find out ways to stay in the status quo?

There are no bad styles; they are just different. Becoming aware of your natural style – and the styles of others – will help you communicate much more effectively. If your style is to talk in visionary "big picture" terms, it will be hard to communicate the complete picture with someone whose natural style is to talk about details and small steps.

Realizing that people come from different perspectives and natural styles of communication and behavior will help you relate your communication to their style. You'll make a real connection with every individual and move the communication forward to a win-win result.

*What is your natural style of communicating?*

Now that you are aware of the differences in natural style, what can you do to bridge the communication gap between you and the other person?

# PART 3
## Powerful questioning and silence will unlock many secrets

*"There is more than a verbal tie between the words common, community, and communication.... Try the experiment of communicating, with fullness and accuracy, some experience to another, especially if it be somewhat complicated, and you will find your own attitude toward your experience changing."*
~ *John Dewey*

Questions give us power. They help level the playing field in business, life, relationships, and success. Questions help us explore and make sense of our world.

Great questions are the most powerful tools we have for changing our lives. Moreover, they allow us to connect with and change the lives of others for the better. They help us gather information, make decisions, remove fear, create solutions, and evolve as spiritual beings in our human experience.

*How can a few words ending with "?" do all that?*

It starts with an inquisitive mind, passion, and intention to seek out new information and new perspectives.

Practice and patience building the skill of asking great questions- ones that make people think and moves ideas forward lets you stand in the space of all possibilities.

Learn to ask questions without judgment or an attachment to the answer. Asking purely for the purpose of hearing the answer. Then explore what ideas the answer creates makes the "**?**" so powerful.

When you can ask a question without judgment and attachment- and listen to the possibilities that the answer creates- you have learned to ask great questions. This will dramatically improve your communication skills, open up new possibilities, and expand your vision of the *soul of success.*

### Why do we use Powerful Questions?
- Gather new information and insights; keep us focused
- Develop a rapport and make genuine connections
- Help people recognize how emotions distort perception
- Help people get out of their head and move into their heart
- Help people hear what they are thinking about

### What do Powerful Questions do?
- Make the people asking and being asked the question think
- Offer new perspectives
- Encourage thoughtful answers and shifts in focus
- Reveal what buttons can be pushed and why
- Honor an individual's intelligence and empower self-discovery

### What are the potential results of Powerful Questions?
- Slow down automatic thinking and reactive responses
- Require you to think "out of the box"
- Illuminate patterns in perceptions and behavior
- Begin to remove the power of the inner critic and limiting beliefs
- Simulate creativity and self-esteem

**_What are some categories of Powerful Questions?_**
- Situational Questions
- Inquiry Questions
- Action Questions
- Feeling Questions
- Rhetorical Questions
- Informative Questions
- Probing Questions
- Serendipity Questions
- Goal Setting Questions
- Reality checking Questions
- Options Questions
- Focusing Questions
- Reflective Questions
- Motivating Questions

It's important to become aware of how internal self-talk can sabotage us simply by the way we ask ourselves questions. Listening to the language of a question – the types of words or inflection used – will unlock the perspective from which they come.

Listening for the way a question is phrased will tell you about the inner dialogue. Do the questions come from a negative or positive frame of reference? Is the glass half full or half empty?

Remember our natural strength in communication comes from using our six senses to communicate the complete picture. You will hear someone use one of their senses to relate an experience. By using their language style and incorporating the same sense in your response, you can make a stronger connection with that person.

_Examples :_
- _I feel so confident (intuition)_
- _I hear myself getting more energetic (auditory)_
- _I am beginning to smell success (olfactory)_
- _It touched my heart (tactile)_
- _Can you see what I mean? (visual)_

- *It left a bad taste in my mouth (taste)*

Using the examples above, we can use the sensory cues to phrase a question that relates to the way language is used. This approach allows you or someone else to fully relate to the question.

*Examples:*
- *How do you feel about this?*
- *What do you see happening here?*
- *How do you picture this?*
- *What did you hear in this?*
- *In what ways will this touch your life?*
- *What are you hungry to accomplish?*

Your voice is like a fine-tuned musical instrument. The tone and quality of your voice are the pieces of music. How you capitalize on it makes a difference in how you are heard.

Following are some questions to consider when thinking about how your voice quality detracts or enhances your communication skills:
- What is the tone and what impact does it have?

- What is the rate of speech and what impact does it have?

- What is the pace and rhythm and what influences does it have?

- Is there nuance in the inflection and what impact does it have?

- What is the source of energy behind the words and what impact does it have?

- What quality of pitch does the voice hold and what influences does it have?

There are two ways to improve your communication skills when asking questions.

1. Listen to the language of the <u>Other Person</u>, including the types of words and inflection that he or she uses.

2. Listen to the language that <u>You</u> use when thinking or talking to yourself, including the types of words and inflection you use.

These two approaches are powerful tools to build confidence, remove doubt, and take action. These tools will help you build momentum and move you forward.

Changing the perspective we question from will change the answers we get. The quality of the answers we give will change the quality of the actions we take. Changing the quality of the actions we take will dramatically improve the quality of the results we get.

It's all a matter of choice and it starts with us, our choice to listen to the inner critic or Wisdom's Voice. It's our choice to use positive or negative language in the way we phrase questions we ask others and ourselves.

Once we improve the quality of the questions we ask ourselves, we can then improve the quality of the questions we ask others. It will help them to quiet the inner critic and tap into Wisdom's Voice.

Taking the small actions necessary to improve the quality of our questions will bring dramatic results.

## STEP 6

### Leveraging connections creating community

*"Without passion life has no meaning. So put your heart, mind, and soul into even your smallest acts... This is the essence of passion. This is the secret to life."*

~ *Anonymous*

The first five steps of this book have taken you on a journey of discovery – looking out with awareness and looking in with a clear, conscious perspective. I hope you have taken the time to work through the exercises, expanding upon them when needed and changing them to suit your particular situation.

Perhaps you have actively read and worked through the steps up to this point. Or maybe you have simply read the book and pondered along the way. In either case, it's the right pace for you at the moment. Consciously choosing the pace and level of action you take working through the book is an important step. Remember to choose that pace because it is a comfortable stretch for you.

Making the commitment to yourself to read this book and actively experience the exercises will move you forward to the *soul of success* with greater momentum. If you are just reading and pondering the exercises, make sure it's because you intuitively know that is the best pace for you at this moment – not because fear, skepticism or being stuck is the motivating factor.

Step 6 is a strategy for bringing community and fellowship into your life. You will discover who you are and what connections would give you the most support. Community is vital to the *soul of success*.

*What does community mean to you?  Who would be the best people to develop fellowship with so you could really share your gifts?*

I believe most definitions of community are too rigid.  Usually, they are structured and defined in the finite physical world rather than a confluence of the spiritual, natural, and intellectual realms.

My definition of community is having shared experiences. It's the act of connecting – a convergence of experiences and ideas. The size, structure or location is not important to my notion of community. It can be large organized communities or small, informal ones.

Communities can be active – places where you meet regularly and have many shared experiences over a long period of time. On the other hand, they can also be passive or inactive. Because my definition of community is having shared experiences, it can be a group of people that you see or interact with only occasionally or only once.

What I have come to know is that by actively leveraging connections and building community, we can connect limitless possibilities with measurable results. These possibilities hold astonishing opportunities for you and for others in the community. More importantly, consciously choosing your communities allows you to share your gifts and give more of yourself.

One of my greatest personal discoveries was realizing that I was a "community of one" made up of many voices with many shared experiences. In this community, the key voices were Wisdom's Voice, my inner critic, Limiting Beliefs, positive role models, and cosmic intuition.

Because I never consciously chose or appreciated the potential of this community, it was a very unhealthy place for me to be. My community of one was governed by negative voices. Nevertheless, as the saying goes – wherever you go, there you are, for better or worse – I was an active, albeit and unconscious member in my community of one.

Awareness of my community of one brought about the conscious choice to become an active member. It took me a long time to master my community of one, but it was the single most important thing I had done in my life up to that point. It was more important than my businesses, my relationships with others, more important than raising my daughter.

Mastering my community of one was so important because it colored and affected everything else I did. Being a conscious active member in my community of one changed my perspective and changed my life.

I had more confidence and greater awareness of others and myself. I was able to communicate and really connect with other people and other communities. Most importantly, I was able to share with my daughter the wonderful gift of modeling how to actively be a part of a community of one in a healthy, meaningful way.

What practical applications does this definition of community offer, especially in helping you achieve the *soul of success*? I offer it to challenge your current notions on community. I would like to you be aware of the connections you make and the sense of community you hold.

I would like you to explore the power of the community of one and its potential negative and positive influences on your life. I see it as a way to bring communion into people's lives and make the path to the *soul of success* much easier.

It is important to begin by looking inward on the question of building community and fellowship. Why? Because we need to know who we are before we can find a community or develop a fellowship that will support and nurture us. We need to have a sense of place, so we can tap into our strengths and make a powerful contribution to our communities of choice.

Many of the communities we belong to now are relationships of convenience or places we chose while still riding the "should express". Instead of building us up, they may be tearing us down. They are standing in our way of mastering the art of riding the seesaw to the *soul of success*.

Tapping into Wisdom's Voice and your brilliance will give you a place in the most powerful community of all – the one you can always count on. It's the one that

has the potential to be your biggest support system, cheerleader, and confidant.
*It's YOURSELF – your community of one.*

You can build fellowship and a sense of community with yourself by spending time on the following:

- Know yourself.
- Reclaim your personal power.
- Discover your uniqueness as an individual and what you can bring to community.
- Recognize your union with a passion and purpose greater than yourself.
- Understand that everything is connected. In order to make our desired changes, we must start with a community of one within ourselves.

### Case Study: Growing and Moving Forward Can Shift Your Communities

Pamela had been coaching with me for about a year. She wanted to focus on growing her business and growing herself. She came to coaching because of a concept she heard at a seminar for entrepreneurs. The speaker said that most small business fail because the owners failed to grow themselves.

Pamela had been doing everything traditionally attributed to success, such as participating in business courses and hiring a bookkeeper. However, she still wasn't happy with her business. Working together, we developed strategies and systems to make her business run more smoothly and become financially efficient. We also focused on Pamela growing herself – what she wanted her business to do for her, as well as the strengths and Limiting Beliefs that she brought to the business.

The communities she belonged to were a drain on her personally and professionally. After matching her "Community Characteristics" and top inner values to each community, she realized why she felt she had so little support. Pamela listed her communities in the following order:

1.    Herself
2.    Associations and networking groups
3.    Business colleagues
4.    Friends

The work Pamela had done growing her business and herself had changed her definition of community-what she was looking for in the communities she belonged to.

Pamela realized she had never consciously chosen her communities. With an awareness of the definition of community as shared experiences, she realigned her list of communities and the impact they had on her life.

#### ---- Exercise ----

### Your Community Characteristics

This exercise helps ensure that the communities that you spend time with – and the ones you connected to – are moving you forward to the *soul of success*. It is important to develop YOUR Community Characteristics.

Essentially, this exercise helps answer the following question: *What are you looking for in the people and organizations you want to have community and fellowship with?*

1.    Start by reviewing your needs and values:

•    First, review your top five needs from Step 3. These needs will be helpful guides in building your community characteristics.

•    Next, list your top five inner values from Step 3. Make sure that the communities you are already a part of are in alignment with these inner values.

2.    Take an "energy reading" next time you are
      participating in your existing communities. As you
      perform the following ratings assessment, be sure to
      tap into how you are feeling and what you may be
      sensing or noticing on an intuitive level.

      On a scale of 1-10 (10 being the best) The following
      rating system on every community you are associated
      with- especially if you are not certain the community is
      really supporting you.

      • Rate how enthusiastic you are about getting
        together with this group (one of your communities).

      • Rate your level of concern over what you are going
        to wear or what others might think of you.

      • Rate your level of friendliness to the people in the
        group.

      • Rate your satisfaction with the pace that the group
        works on activities you are passionate about.

      • Rate the level of anxiety you may experience when
        thinking what you are going to chat about with the
        other people in the group.

      • Is there someone in the group that has hurt your
        feelings or just gives you a bad "vibe"? Rate your
        level of focus and judgment towards this person.

      • Rate your level of energy before meeting with the
        group.

      • Rate your level of energy while you are with the
        group.

      • Rate your level of energy a ½ hour after being with
        the group.

Make a list of the characteristics of your ideal community and
its members.

      *Example:*
      • *Everyone is actively involved.*

- *They are friendly.*
- *People always seem to be learning and sharing experiences.*
- *There is a willingness to collaborate.*
- *I feel safe there.*
- *The group gives me great ideas.*
- *The group is diverse.*
- *I am always learning something new.*
- *People have different opinions but respect mine.*
- *I feel like I can really contribute something to this group.*
- *The group is open to new people.*
- *Being involved with this group really supports two of my inner values.*

3.    You have listed your Community's Characteristics and thought about which ones are important to you. Now answer the following questions to match your new insights with any community you may already be a part of:

- Is this community a good fit for you?

- What could you shift or change to make this community support all of your top inner values?

- If this community isn't really a good fit, what is it that keeps you coming back?

- Is there someone in the community that is a good fit? Would you be willing to see if other communities they are involved with may be a better fit?

--------

## PART 1

### Be open to the gifts of synchronicity

*"There is no end. There is no beginning. There is only
the infinite passion of life." ~ Frederico Fellini*

Psychiatrist Carl Jung defined synchronicity as
"meaningful coincidence:"

I don't believe in coincidences so I like to think
of synchronicity as being awake and aware of
ourselves and our environment. Attuned to the gifts
and signs that are always showing up to help move us
forward.

### Case Study: Hearing Songs; Musical Synchronicity

Jan was getting over the breakup of her marriage
and getting back on her feet seemed to be going really
slowly.

We were coaching together on this major life
transition as well as looking at her career. Jan was
frustrated because she felt she had worked through
many unresolved issues from her marriage with
Terrence. However, she still didn't feel free and able to
move forward with her life.

I asked her to think of what could be standing in
the way of moving forward. Blocked by her frustration,
Jan could not see any specific thing blocking her path.
She agreed to tune into the Universe and use
synchronicity as a guide in finding the answer of what
was blocking her. What showed up for Jan was a series
of songs that unlocked the key to unresolved issues.

One song reminded Jan of her first date with
Terrance and a little nagging feeling she had about him.
Another song had lyrics that spoke to Jan's insecurities
around earning money.

Jan heard 10 songs in two days that pointed out
areas she hadn't really resolved yet. Some were directly

connected to her relationship with Terrence, but most highlighted areas in her own life she still wanted to work on.

"Hearing" these songs and seeing their message of synchronicity lifted the frustration from Jan. She had some things to resolve and think about. However, the shift in perspective that the musical synchronicity gave her removed the struggle and frustration. This shift in perspective allowed her to move forward with her new life.

Jan shared the following quote from Rick Jarow, which helped her open up to more instances of synchronicity: "Living in relationship to everything and everyone, that's the greatest practice that will open synchronicity. Being totally inclusive. Anything that happens, you relate to it – if your three-year-old comes in and says something, if a rock comes in the window. You live in relationship with everything and everyone. A relationship to me means you're not judgmental. You're not removing yourself. You're vulnerable. You're exposing yourself to the universe. There's no distance."

#### ---- Exercise ----

#### Synchronicity Awareness Quiz

For each of the following questions, place a checkmark in the box every time your answer is "yes":

❑      Have you ever thought about someone...and then received a call from this individual after you were thinking about him or her?

❑      Have you ever been running late...and then the traffic clears or train arrives early so you arrive right on time?

❑      Have you been short a few dollars...and then found just the right amount of money hidden in your coat pocket or purse?

❑   Have you found yourself in a hurry to an event or movie and become focused on finding a parking space...and then one opens up right in front of your destination?

❑   Have you ever been looking for a sign or answer to a problem... and not only get the answer but also someone to help you put the solution into place?

❑   Have you ever thought about a friend...and then ran into this person unexpectedly?

❑   Have you been looking for ways to market your business... and then creative solutions unexpectedly appear?

❑   Have you been thinking about networking....and then run into several people who offer you opportunities to promote yourself?

❑   Have you written down an idea or clearly defined something you want...and then it materializes for you?

❑   Do you remember a time when there were many obstacles in your way... but they eventually led you to change direction to a much better path?

❑   Have you had your questions answered by strangers or a talk show guest on a radio program you are listening to before you consciously asked the question?

❑   Do you see a pattern of meaningful coincidence validating the direction you are moving in?

Tally the number of boxes that you checked. Now compare this number to the following rating scale to assess your synchronicity:

0-3     You are not awake to the gifts of synchronicity. Picking up this book is a sign you are ready to be more aware and in touch with synchronicity.

4-7     You are aware of synchronicity, but you don't trust it yet. Your skepticism blocks more of it from flowing into your life.

8-11    You consciously look for sign of synchronicity, and you are actively looking for signs.

12      You are living in the moment and actively attracting synchronicity into your life to create success on your own terms.

--------

## Case Study: Running into Opportunities

Nola was working with me on marketing and networking to expand her business. She had a very analytical mind and liked systems and structure in running her business. This natural style had served her well for setting up business systems, but it wasn't effective with marketing and networking her business.

I requested that she look for synchronicity to point the way to good networking opportunities. She could then use it as a tool to help her choose more successful marketing vehicles.

At first, she felt great resistance and uncertainty toward this request. Nola couldn't see how leaving things up to chance or guessing about where to market could help her business. In fact, she was very nervous about the possible negative consequences that this approach might have on her business.

Six weeks later – and still very skeptical – Nola finally agreed to be open to synchronicity. First, we focused on networking. Nola wanted to promote her accounting business by giving presentations, but she wasn't sure of the best place to start. I asked her to write an "Intention Statement" for running into opportunities that would give her great networking and marketing outlets.

**Nola's Intention statement:**
*In the next 10 days, I intend to find two people who can support me in growing my business. I will be able to leverage these connections into networking opportunities and ways to show the value of my services rather than trying to sell them.*

Although still uncertain about how this exercise would work for her, she agreed and focused on her Intention Statement three times a day.

Nola called me just two days after writing her Intention Statement. She was fired up! She had just come back from running a few errands. While running her errands, Nola booked three networking engagements and found a terrific place to market her services. Nola confessed that she was much more open to these new opportunities – and the synchronicity that brought them to her – because she had really focused on her Intention Statement. She decided to become open to the possibilities that the Universe was ready to offer her.

Nola explained that she had posted her Intention Statement several places in her home and office. Every time that she saw it, Nora read the statement aloud. While reading her Intention Statement, she thought about networking and marketing opportunities coming to her.

#### ---- Exercise ----

#### How to Write an Intention Statement

When you write an Intention Statement, you are focusing on something you want to happen. *You aren't sure HOW it will happen. However, you are sure it WILL happen.* You have an open mind to the opportunities that will come to you to make it happen.

1.      The following three steps will help you become clear about what you want, so you can write a powerful Intention Statement:

- Write what you want to accomplish or have happen. *Example: In the next two weeks, I want to find two excellent networking opportunities to grow my business.*

- Write why you want to accomplish or open up to this opportunity. *Example: I want to have these networking opportunities, so I can make connections with interesting people and provide my new clients with excellent service.*

- Describe what it will feel like once this happens. *Example: I will feel very proud of myself for getting out there and making new friends...and I will have a sense of satisfaction from taking action to grow my business.*

2.  Now combine your responses to the above three questions into an Intention Statement.

    *Example: In the next two weeks, I intend to find two new networking opportunities that put me in contact with interesting people and my ideal clients.*

There are two important things to remember when writing your Intention Statement:

- Keep it positive and direct.

- Read your Intention Statement aloud and imagine what it will feel like when you bring these things into your life.

--------

### *Case Study: Asking for Guidance*

Tom was looking for a new department head, but he was having trouble finding someone who really fit the job responsibilities. He posted several notices within the company and contacted a few recruitment services. However, he couldn't find a person with the right energy and sense of vision to grow the new department strategically and effectively.

I asked Tom if he ever noticed evidence of the gift of synchronicity in his life. He said it had showed up for him in small ways, but not in any real pronounced ways. He was willing to make an Intention Statement around finding the right person and developing his skill of being more open to hearing guidance from the Universe.

Along with the other things we were working on Tom practiced his openness to Universal guidance. Over the next month, he noticed a big difference in the opportunities that seemed to flow effortlessly into his life.

Tom hadn't written an Intention Statement on the new position yet. He was still too attached to the outcome. Tom felt he was focusing too much energy on not having someone in the position rather than having someone who would be perfect for the position.

I requested that Tom write a detailed ad for the person he was looking for – including specifics about what that person enjoyed doing out of the office and what special skills he or she would bring to the job that Tom hadn't even considered yet.

He posted the ad several places in the office and at home. He never ran it in the newspaper or job listing service; he just put it out to the Universe. Two weeks later, Tom had interviewed two people who were perfect for the position. He asked them to share what they thought the job outcomes should be for their vision of what could be accomplish by having this new position.

He ended up hiring both of them and making some strategic changes in the company that resulted in expanded profits and a much better working environment.

#### ---- Exercise ----

### Listening for Guidance and Synchronicity

This exercise will help you start every day with the intent to be open to synchronicity and guidance when it shows up in your life.

Start by taking a 5-10 minute meditation break to quiet your mind and the "To-Do" list that seems to be constantly running.

- Close your eyes and just observe your thoughts.

- Be flexible and spontaneous. LISTEN when Wisdom's Voice whispers to you. Then ACTUALLY STOP AND HAVE A CONVERSATION WITH IT.

- Ask for signs that you are moving in the right path.

- Be open to the gifts in the events of synchronicity you encounter.

--------

## PART 2

### Building your community builds your success

*"There are precious few Einsteins among us.*
*Most brilliance arises from ordinary people working together in*
*extraordinary ways." ~ Roger von Oech*

Some of the most profound experiences I've had were with a community of strangers. The first whale watch I ever went on taught me how you could have communion with strangers and a true sense of community.

We set out from Martha's Vineyard to Stellwagen Bank looking for humpback whales. It was an overcast morning with a stiff breeze, but we were determined to have an adventure and see some whales.

The fog was so thick you couldn't even see the wake of the boat. The sky and water were the same flat gray, which made it hard to tell were the sea ended and the horizon began.

We became a community of strangers all hoping for the same thing – to see whales. The mood on the boat was split. Some people were optimistic and peered through the gray mists scanning for the slicing of a dorsal fin through the water and intently listening for the sound of spray from a blowhole. Other people were consumed by the vast churning gray ocean and the doubt of finding anything but more open sea.

Then, like the mists of Avalon, the sky opened up and the seas quieted. We were surrounded by whales. It was magnificent. The whales seemed as interested in us as we were in them. The stretch of water around the boat was teaming with dolphins, humpbacks, minkies, and fin backs.

One humpback came alongside the boat and rolled to take a nice long pan of the people along the port side. She was so close that you could see every detail of her large, warm eye. We seemed to be a source of joy and amusement to her. One exuberant juvenile humpback miscalculated his play and bumped the boat.

Then the sky closed in and the sea began to churn. We steamed home in the most miserable weather imaginable. Nonetheless, the mood on the boat seemed reverent.

As we left the boat and walked back to our cars, I felt a real connection with these people. Together, we saw 75 Atlantic white sided dolphins, 35 humpback whales, 4 minkie whales, and 2 fin back whales. We had become a community of strangers and our incredible experience that day would stay with us forever.

That shared experience had a profound effect on my community of one. It gave me tools and new perspective for making connections with people and becoming comfortable quickly in new settings.

"Connection Networking" is vital to achieving the *soul of success*. I'm not talking about the events where you put on a name tag and wander around a sterile reception room hoping to make a few good contacts.

I am talking about building a network that supports your success, both the doing and the being of it. Building a network of people with common interests and expansive views, people you can form deep connections with. Whether you talk to people in this network regularly or only once a year, you are connected on an energetic level. With Connection Networking, there is a resonance to the relationship that is mutually supportive.

I build on my relationships by staying in touch in effortless ways. I may forward a resource via email, send a fun card, call occasionally for a virtual lunch or follow their accomplishments and acknowledge them for it.

There is a real connection to the relationship, but it's effortless and without obligation. Because of this flow in the relationship, we easily attract referrals and ideal opportunities for each other.

Are you uncomfortable with the conventional approach to networking? If you're answer is "yes," Connection Networking can improve your relationships and success. It's time to get out there and make connections!

How do you begin to incorporate Connection Networking into your life? The following exercise helps you stretch your comfort level in small ways.

#### ---- Exercise ----

#### Be Self-Reliant and Stretch Your Comfort Level

**Definition of Being Self-Reliant:** Reliance upon one's own capabilities, judgment or resources. Self-reliance stresses self-trust manifested in action. It implies independence and self-sufficiency.

Write answers to the following questions in your journal, notebook, or computer file.

• What things did you do when you were younger that you would not have the courage to try now?

• What is keeping you stuck in the same routine every week?

- What new things are you hesitant to try?

  When you hear yourself saying, "I always wanted to try that," what would it be like for you to try it this time?

  *Example: Every now and then, I find myself retracting. Becoming hesitant to try something new or do something I used to do again. I don't like that feeling. I get annoyed at myself for being wimpy, for not paying attention to what is important to me. I am aware of this bad habit and catch myself when I am spending time second-guessing myself, listing all the reasons why I shouldn't do something. Do not "should" yourself out of a rich meaningful life.*

Now is the time to stretch your self-reliance muscles to expand your comfort level. I challenge you to try at least five of the suggestions below to stretch your boundaries in the next two weeks. Then I challenge you to get started on the things you have always wanted to try.

- Take a course at your local high school adult education center or community college.
- Volunteer at the council on aging.
- Try a new sport like in-line skating or mountain biking.
- Take a different route to and from work for a week.
- Buy a shirt in a color you don't normally wear.
- Order something new on the menu at your favorite restaurant.
- Volunteer to read to children at your local library or grade school.
- Eat at a new ethnic restaurant.
- Become part of a mentor program.
- Eat lunch by yourself.
- Go to a lecture or topic you are not familiar with.
- Attend a spiritual workshop.
- Make an effort to be more understanding of someone you don't like.
- Get to know the people in your neighborhood.
- Do something nice for someone just because.
- Spend one day in non-judgment. Begin the day saying " I will judge nothing that occurs today."

--------

## PART 3
## Leveraging full circle perspective

*"How far you go in life depends on your being tender
with the young, compassionate with the aged, sympathetic
with the striving and tolerant of the weak and the strong.
Because someday in life you will have been all of these."*
~ *George Washington Carver*

The *soul of success* is all about dancing with the
two components of success – DOING OF SUCCESS and
BEING OF SUCCESS. Leveraging full circle perspective
makes dancing with those components much easier.

The idea is to stand with yourself and your
business or career in the center of action. You then
visualize all of your thoughts, actions, and feelings
radiating out from that center and forming connections.

Some connections will be of a "doing" nature and
some will be of a "being" nature. With this full circle
perspective, you can leverage all of your actions to pull
you forward to create success on your own terms. You
will find that using full circle perspective breaks the
inertia and feeling of overwhelm and being stuck. It will
remove the idea of not having a choice in your life.

Small achievements will help you gain
momentum. Each step forward will give you more
confidence and build your momentum towards the *soul
of success*.

### Key strategies for leveraging full circle perspective

Take a look at the one and only person
responsible for your success – YOU. In order to be
successful, you must take complete responsibility for
your actions. You can't pin your success or your
shortcomings on anyone else.

It is important to develop and nurture a
successful self. Start by smiling more. Look to the

positive side in everything. Do not list all the reasons
why something is hard and you can't do it. Instead, find
the reasons – even if there is only one – why you can do
something.

You must develop a successful persona to become
a successful person. Start with a commitment to
yourself. Make the decision today. Decide today that
you will be successful. Praise yourself for past
accomplishments, take stock of your strengths, and find
ways to minimize or delegate any weaknesses.

You have a purpose and a mission. You must
sweep aside the negative clutter. Define this purpose.
And fulfill yourself starting today.

Always begin with the positive- every morning you
wake up and every time you speak with other people.
Always stick with the positive. Associate with positive
people – people who have also made the commitment to
success.

Avoid negative people at all costs. They will only
drag you down. Their negative actions and thoughts –
their pessimism, whining, and complaining – are toxins
you need to steer clear of.

Visualize and write down how you desire to live
successfully. Think of the things that are meaningful to
you – those things that give you pleasure, comfort, and
fulfillment. Then being as specific as possible, write
down how you want to live. Don't listen to any of the
negative, just concentrate.

You will need a journal or notebook with blank
pages for this exercise. Write down every detail: where
you live; what your house is like down to the décor; what
you and your friends are passionate about; what kinds of
community projects you give donations of time and
money; what you want your business or career to do for
you, capturing both the financial and intangible sides.

Make the journal come to life with drawings,
photographs, magazine clippings, articles, and poetry.
Incorporate images and words that will help your vision
of a successful life crystallize in your mind. Spend five
minutes every day visualizing mastering the art of riding

the seesaw of success. Make all of your actions in accordance with achieving the *soul of success*.

Define what success means to you. Concentrate on what you are best at and what brings you satisfaction and fulfillment. Using your vision of how you want to live, write down – and then read aloud – what success means to you. Otherwise, you won t know when you have achieved it.

Study and make the commitment. Read books and magazines about people who are successful in your eyes, in addition to ways to become more successful. Develop a daily systematic approach to reaching your goals and take one step towards your success. Keep your mind in the moment; don't let it wander to negative discourse. Focus your attention on your vision of success. With a resolute attitude, you are well on your way.

*"The longer I live, the more I realize the impact of attitude on life. Attitude to me is more important than facts. It is more important than the past, than education, than money, than circumstances, than failures, than success, than what other people think or say or do. It is more important than appearance, gift, or skill. It will make or break a company...a church...a home. The remarkable thing is we have a choice every day regarding the attitude we will embrace for that day. We cannot change our past...we cannot change the fact that people will act in a certain way. We cannot change the inevitable. The only thing we can do is play on the string we have, and that is our attitude. I am convinced that life is 10 percent what happens to me and 90 percent how I react to it. And so it is with you... we are in charge of our attitudes."*
                                    *~ Charles Swindoll*

## STEP 7
## Rising to challenges, staying the course

*"Challenges make you discover things about yourself
that you never really knew. They're what make the instrument
stretch – what make you go beyond the norm."*
˜ *Cicely Tyson*

Why is it that we can read a "self-help" book then
become inspired and feel motivated to create success on
our own terms yet still feel stuck ?

### ---- Exercise ----
### Morning Garbage Pages

My clients find this exercise to be very helpful and enlightening.
It clears away mind clutter, the layers and layers of "shoulds",
endless lists, mindless chatter, and the sharp edge of Limiting
Beliefs.

This exercise should be done first thing in the morning.  It will
only take about 10 minutes and it will give you a feeling of
adding two hours to your day!  So make the time to do this
exercise and enjoy how great you feel with all of the new time
you have.

Use sheets of paper that are at least 5" x 8" for this exercise.  A
full sheet of paper is even better.

First thing in the morning, I want you to completely fill three
sides of paper by writing from top to bottom. Write whatever
comes to mind.  Don't leave any blank space.

### *Tips for Completing This Exercise:*
*   Don't edit.
*   Don't worry about spelling or grammar.
*   Remember that no one else will see this exercise.
*   If you can't think of anything, just write "I can't think of
    anything to write yet!"

- Let all of your nagging thoughts, endless lists, etc. spill onto the paper.
- Keep writing and don't stop.
- Just let your thoughts flow onto the paper.
- Don't stop to read what you have written.
- Burn, shred or crumple the pages once you have finished writing them.  Throw them away.

Write your morning garbage pages every day for at least two weeks.

--------

### Case Study: Clearing Your Mind Lets Ideas Flow

Perrine was a successful attorney who was in line for a partnership with a caseload of interesting clients. Although things were moving along right on track, she felt like something was definitely missing.

Perrine loved the law – all of its intricacies and the satisfaction of making the complex simple and easy to grasp.  However, she was distracted and discouraged. She was about to become a partner in the firm yet being a lawyer wasn't giving her any energy.

She woke up tired every day and left the office even more tired every night.  She felt like a drone just going through paper work, hearing her clients talk but not being able to really listen.

I asked Perrine to use the "Morning Garbage Pages" exercise as a way to clear all of her mind clutter. Getting past the clutter would make it easier for Perrine to see if being a lawyer and a partner were still important to her.

The first few days, she wrote the usual stuff – a lot of "shoulds" and endless lists of things to do.  By the fourth day, Perrine found herself letting go of a lot of thoughts and worries she didn't even realize she had been holding on to.

Perrine gave a lot of thought to her work as a lawyer. Writing the "Morning Garbage Pages" freed her up to think about what she wanted her career to do for her and what she wanted to give to people by being a lawyer.

She decided that a partnership – at least in the firm she was currently in – was not the right choice for her. Perrine wanted to keep practicing law. However, she wanted to find a way to do it that worked for her – not just working longer and harder to get ahead in a direction that didn't really suit her.

Perrine found the exercise so useful that she continues to write her "Morning Garbage Pages" every day. It keeps her mind clear and lets her focus on what's really important to her.

## PART 1

### Focus on what you want, not what you don't want

> *"Our greatest glory is not in never failing,*
> *but in rising up every time we fail."*
> *~ Ralph Waldo Emerson*

Our thoughts and feelings create our reality. Step 1 was about coming to consciousness – becoming aware of your thoughts and feelings and consciously creating what you want.

Why do we run into struggle staying the course? Because even though we are conscious, we still don't seem to be creating what we want in our lives. Often, we are focusing our energy on what we don't want instead of what we really want. It usually occurs without our awareness. We add a negative perspective to a phrase. We think we are focusing on what we want, but our words and thoughts are really focusing on the lack and our wanting.

An example would be someone who wants to lose weight. This person focuses on wanting to be thin. What this brings to mind in thoughts and feelings is "I am not thin, I'm heavy and I don't like being this way." Another example is when we want to bring more money into our lives. Often, we pinch pennies. However, this approach makes us focus on our lack. We say things like, "I can't afford to buy that or I never have enough money to do what I want."

Whatever we focus our thoughts and attention and amplify with our feelings is what we bring into our lives. It's a Universal law. It's the Law of Attraction.

Simply put, the Law of Attraction states that you attract to your life whatever you give your attention, feelings, focus, energy, and intention to – whether it is wanted or unwanted.

Sometimes, my clients become frustrated because they have reached a plateau. They have made great shifts in their personal growth and become aware of what they really want out of life. However, they don't seem to be moving forward.

They have planted many seeds through networking to open up new opportunities yet nothing seems to be sprouting. They are "doing" everything right but still that "forward momentum" – *the feeling of accomplishment and success* – eludes them.

When this happens to my clients, it's because they are focusing on what they don't want instead of what they want. Following are a few ways to change this:

1.    Make sure your thoughts and language are positive. Don't say, "I hate my job, I need a change." Instead, say something like "I am really ready for a change of pace, I want a job I love." You have essentially said the same thing yet the emotional energy you are sending out when you say it is very different. In the first statement, you are focusing on what you don't want. In second statement, you are focusing on what you want.

2.    Make sure you are clear about what you really want, why it's important to you and most of all what it will feel like when you get it. Keep your thoughts and language positive. Use the intense feelings of fun, pleasure, satisfaction, pride- all these feelings that accomplishment of the goal will

bring. As you speak the words to describe what
you wan feel those emotions. This will make your
words more powerful

3.     Make sure to choose your mood and how you
       react to things. Have you ever noticed when you
       are excited, doing well, and on a successful roll
       you tend to attract more success towards you.
       This is the Law of Attraction. It feels great
       because you are attracting things that you want
       into your life. I am sure you have been in a place
       where everything seems to be going from bad to
       worse. Your thoughts and language are focusing
       on what's going wrong. You have strong feelings
       of discomfort – perhaps even fear – about what's
       going on. Again, the Law of Attraction is at work
       in these situations.

**Case Study: Turning Thoughts Into Energy That
Creates Actions and Results**

       Loraine didn't believe in the energy of thought
until we spent a whole week consciously attracting
specific things. We started with a few very simple ideas
and explored bringing both negative and positive things
into her life.
       Loraine didn't get along with her brother-in-law
Evin. He always seemed to be down on everything she
did. Before she went to visit her sister, Loraine would
think about him. She focused on the negative things
that Evin had said or done the last time she was at the
house.
       Remembering these visits made her relive her
feelings of being left out and isolated from her sister. She
was frustrated because no matter what she did she just
couldn't get Evin to like her.
       In two days, Loraine would be having dinner with
her sister and Evin. So we used this occasion as the
perfect opportunity to experiment with turning thoughts
and feelings into outcomes. I asked Loraine to

concentrate on what she liked about Evin. Loraine responded that Evin made her sister very happy. Then I asked her to focus on how it made her feel to know her sister had such a happy, loving marriage.

Together with other positive thoughts about Evin, Loraine worked on these ideas over the next two days. She thought of some topics that would make good discussion and keep the conversation positive.

Loraine found that two days of actively thinking about Evin in a positive way made her excited about going to her sister's house for dinner. Instead of the usual fuss over what to wear to avoid a negative comment, Loraine was relaxed and put on her favorite slacks and sweater.

This time Loraine, arrived a little early for dinner. She was looking forward to the evening instead of dreading it like she had so many times before. Much to her surprise, Evin seemed to emulate the relaxed mood that she felt. The conversation was pleasant, even fun.

Impressed with the results of this first experiment, Loraine agreed to consciously use the power of her thoughts and feelings to create the changes she wanted to make in her career.

Things didn't change overnight. But slowly, Loraine got in the habit of focusing on the positive side of situations. She looked at things she wanted to accomplish and got clear on what she wanted to do. Loraine examined what she wanted to accomplish in different situations and what it would feel like when she did. Then she used those strong feelings to help her focus her thoughts and attention to create what she wanted to happen.

---- **Exercise** ----

## Running Energy

My intuition coach, Jennifer, taught me this wonderful exercise of running energy. It is a great way to get you grounded and focused.

Running energy allows you to effortlessly tap into your personal power and Wisdom's Voice. Once you practice this exercise several times in a quiet place with total concentration, you will be able to do it any time. You can run energy while standing in a line at the store...while sitting in your car stuck in traffic... or while waiting for an appointment to become more relaxed and focused.

### *Steps to Running Energy:*

- Sit up straight in a comfortable chair. Make sure the soles of your feet are flat on the floor.

- Close your eyes and relax. Take three deep cleansing breaths.

- Imagine a long root leaving the soles of your feet and going down into the core of the earth.

- Now imagine that cord is sending energy back to you. You can feel a soft, gentle hum, as the healing energy of the earth comes back up the cord into your feet.

- Continue to sit quietly and breathe deeply – just concentrate on tapping this root down deep into the core of the earth. Concentrate on the warm, soft energy that is being sent to you along this cord from the center of the earth.

   *TIP: You will want to practice this step to running energy for a few days. Just get used to the feeling of connection and receiving the earth's energy. Next time you practice running energy, get your grounding cord to go all the way to the center of the earth.*

- Receive the healing energy vibration that comes from the earth. Then concentrate on running that energy for a few minutes.

- Now feel that energy cord expanding like the wide trunk of a magnificent old tree.

- Continue to run energy but let the cord be 6-7 feet wide, so it supports you and your aura (the energy field around your body).

Once you get into the habit of running energy when you are sitting in a quiet place, you can use this same technique while standing or sitting someplace that isn't quiet.

Running energy will help you clear out old pictures from your energy field. These images can be Limiting Beliefs that you have held as an energetic block. Running energy is a great way to clear mental clutter, reduce the chatter from your inner critic, and turn up the volume of your Wisdom's Voice.

Whether you do a lot of mind-body spiritual practices or are skeptical to all this Woo Woo stuff, running energy is simple to do. It is a practical tool for getting more focused and using the power of your thoughts and feelings to create what you want in your life.

--------

## PART 2

### Choose your circles wisely

> *"No one can make you feel inferior without your consent."*
> ~ *Eleanor Roosevelt*

An important tool in rising to challenges and staying the course is choosing your key circles wisely.

## FRIENDS: Your First Key Circle

The first is your circle of friends. Vital to your success is having the genuine loving support of others. You will grow as you move forward to achieving the *soul of success*. As you make shifts in attitude, habits, feelings, and commitments, you may need to make shifts in your circle of friends. Make sure that the friends you have now are ones who support the changes you are making and are not holding you back.

There is a cost to moving forward and creating what you really want in your life and your career. Sometimes that cost comes in the price of having to let old friends go to make room for new friends that really support and guide you in the next phase of your life.

## ROLE MODELS: Your Second Key Circle

Another circle you need to choose wisely is the one that includes people who model what you want to have more of.

You want to include people in this circle who have a strong inner foundation and a sense of self. It can be devastating to include people who have what you want more of but have no integrity or inner values to guide their actions.

If you want to have more money, hanging out with someone who is engaged in corporate fraud or unscrupulous business dealings is not a wise choice for your circle. Someone who is never satisfied with the things they have or the money they have, but needs more just for the sake of having more, is not a wise choice for your circle.

When you see someone you admire, it's because that same quality exists within you. *You cannot admire a quality which you do not already possess.* This understanding will build your confidence and polish your strengths.

Use the awareness of the Law of Attraction to develop a large circle of people that you can learn from.

A circle of people who will support you, challenge you, and hold you accountable to the standards you have for yourself.

## LIFE ENERGY and FOCUS: Your Third Key Circle

The circle of your life energy and focus is the third important one to choose wisely. This circle reflects where you spend your time and life energy. If you say you want to focus on your creative projects but you never make time for them you are not choosing this circle wisely. If you want your business to provide you with time and money so you can travel but you work sixty hours a week and never take time off you are not choosing this circle wisely.

Too often, these circles are poorly chosen and do not reflect how we truly want to be spending our time and energy. Awarness of how the circle currently looks – and our ideal image of this circle – is the first step to feeling balanced and spending your time the way you were meant to.

I have developed a tool called the "Life Matters Wheel" to help you map out or assess these circles. It will help you get a clearer picture of how to choose your circles wisely.

### ---- Exercise ----

### Life Matters Wheels

**How to Complete Your CURRENT Life Matters Wheel:**

1. Select six categories that represent major areas where you spend your time:

   *Examples:*
   *Work - Life Balance*
   *Me (time just for you)*
   *Fun / Travel*
   *Family*
   *Marriage*

*Relationships*
*Lifelong Learning*
*Personal Development*
*Physical Fitness*
*Children*
*Work*

2. Write these six categories in a list on the left, outside of the Life Matters circle shown on the following page. It doesn't matter what order you write them in. Just write each category and leave a space next to it so you can rate it.

3. Write the percentage of time you spend in each category.

   *Example:*
   • *70% = Work – Life Balance*
   • *10% = Me*

4. Now, still working on the list on the left outside of the "Life Matters" circle, rate your satisfaction with each category by writing one of the following:

   • Doing too much
   • Not enough
   • Okay

5. From the center of circle, draw a pie shape that represents the percentage of time you currently spend in each category. This will give you a visual of how you are currently spending your time.

**Example:**

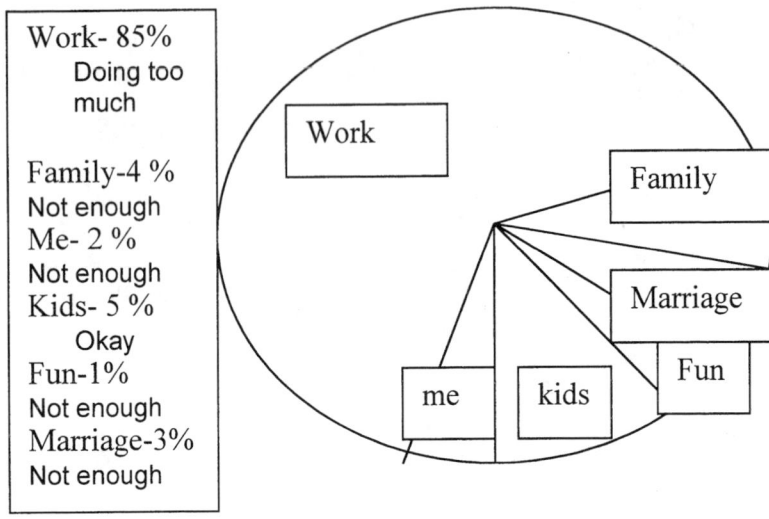

Work- 85%
   Doing too
   much

Family-4 %
Not enough
Me- 2 %
Not enough
Kids- 5 %
   Okay
Fun-1%
Not enough
Marriage-3%
Not enough

## Your Current Life Matters Wheel

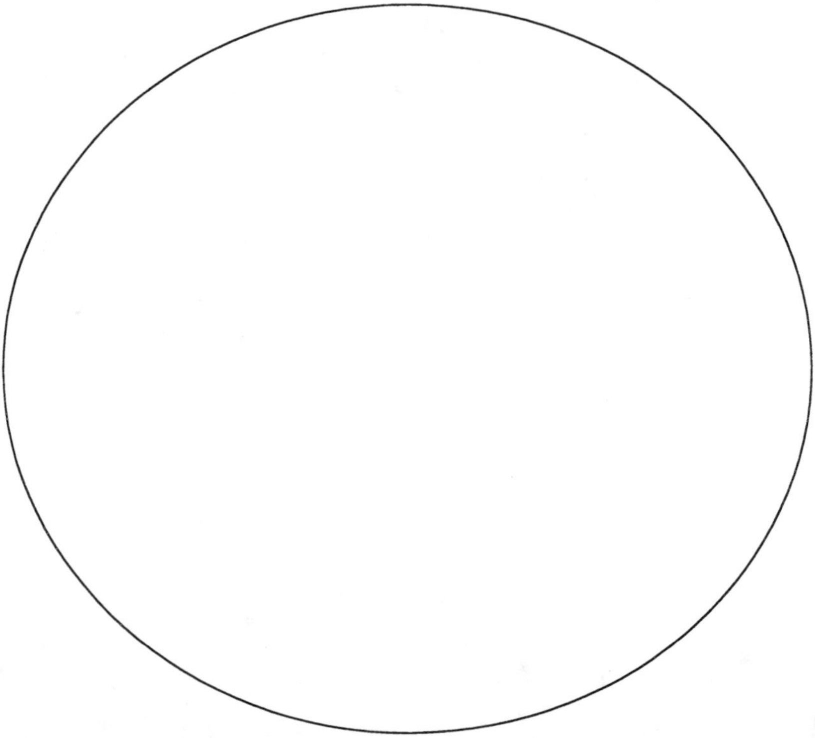

**How to Complete Your IDEAL Life Matters Wheel:**

1.  Review your six categories. Do you need to change any to fit on your IDEAL wheel? You can change the names and drop or add categories to make it reflect your ideal – how you really want to be spending your time.

2.  Write these six categories in a list on the left, outside of the Life Matters circle that appears after these instructions. It doesn't matter what order you write them. Just write each category and leave a space next to it so you can rate it.

3.  Which category would you like to spend the most amount of time in? Write the percentage of time you want to spend in each category.

4.  Using the ideal percentage of time for each category, draw your pie shapes for the ideal wheel.

5.  Compare your CURRENT Life Matters Wheel with your IDEAL Life Matters Wheel. What differences do you see?

6.  Reflect on the difference between the way you are *currently* spending your time and the way you *really want* to spend your time. List six small actions you can take to move to your ideal.

## Your Ideal Life Matters Wheel

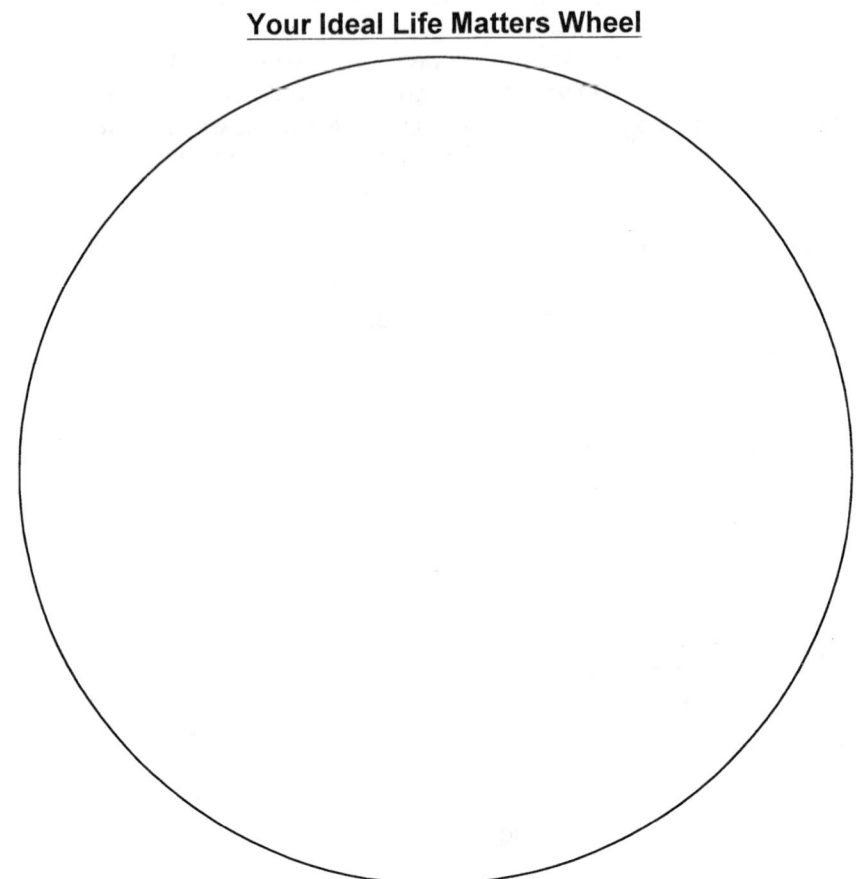

   The "Life Matters Wheel" exercise is valuable
because it provides a visual to illustrate how you are
currently spending your time and how you really want to
spend your time.
   Creating this visual creates awareness. This
awareness will help you understand why you are feeling
stuck, overwhelmed or dissatisfied with things in your
life.

The visual will also shift your perspective on how you spend your time. Often, when we are in denial about something, it is hard for us to see the truth. Creating the visual shows you where your perspective does not meet the current reality of your situation.

### Case Study: Seeing a Clear Picture Helps Shift Perspective

Anne was a workaholic although she couldn't see it clearly. She hired me to get herself more organized. She wanted to use her time more efficiently and productively.

She was just starting a relationship with a wonderful man she met on her first vacation in two years. She wanted to make sure that she used her time with him effectively, too.

Anne saw her life as being hectic, but in complete balance. She just needed to be more organized with her time and then things would really be perfect.

I wanted to have Anne see the difference between what her life was actually like and what she pictured it to be like (if she was only more organized). Before asking her to complete the Life Matters Wheels, we spent some time discussing what was really important to her.

I asked Anne to come up with a set of criteria of: 1) what she thought was a good use of her time; 2) what she felt was part of a fun balanced life, and 3) what she really wanted to spend her leisure and work time doing.

Anne was intrigued by these questions because she thought she was already doing all of these things. She thought they would be easy to put down on paper.

The exercise proved to be much more thought provoking and more difficult. After spending several weeks exploring the questions I asked her. she was ready to do the Life Matters exercise Anne wanted to see a clear visual of her current Life Matters wheel and her ideal Life Matters wheel.

Anne was quite surprised by the visual. She did just a few of the things she said were very important when thinking of her leisure and work time. She also saw a large gap between what she thought was a good use of her time and how she actually spent it.

The Life Matters assessment proved to be a very simple but practical tool to help Anne. She was able to identify what things she could change to make her life work the way she really wanted it to. We did do some work on getting organized, but we started with coaching around Anne being honest with herself and creating what she wanted from her life and work.

# PART 3

## Success comes from you, it doesn't come to you

*"Life shrinks or expands in proportion to one's courage."*
*˜ Anais Ninn*

*Wondering when you will be successful ?*

*Are you waiting for your ship to come in?*

*Are you waiting for that magic meeting with the person who will love your ideas and pay you billions?*

*Are you waiting to be discovered?*

You may be waiting a long time for these things to happen. But you can make these things happen *tomorrow* – if you are willing to get started *TODAY!*

Success comes from YOU. You define it. You create it. You attract synchronicity and other magical things to you. When you decide you are ready for success and you are ready to create the unique success that will fit your heart mind and soul perfectly, you are ready to achive the *soul of success.*

Until you make the decisionto take action- until you put thought, feeling and action behind it- you will be waitng passively for things to come to you. If that is the choice you make, it will be inportant to have a comfortable chair because you will be waiting a long time.

- What is your definition of success?

- What do you want your life and your career to do for you?

When I ask some of my clients these questions, they have a hard time answering. *"I don't know, I want to make money, pay my bills, etc."* These types of comments are not really something to get excited about or work hard for are they?

Other clients respond right away with words like *control, security,* and *more money.* Again, these answers don't really provide the inspiration needed to become creative, use ingenuity or work hard.

These one word responses are often an expression of a need that the client is trying to get met much like the breathing exercise in Step 3. They can't breathe so they can't focus on anything but getting air, in this case air is symbolized by security, control or some other pressing need.

When I first start working with a client, this is one of the very first questions I ask: *"What do you want your business or career to do for you?"*

When we first start coaching together, I don't expect an answer from the client. I just like to ask the question and plant the seed, so the individual starts thinking about the different possibilities. The exercises, assessments, questions and time we spend coaching helps the client to answer the question honestly and thoughtfully.

When the time is right, I will break the question down to a more narrow focus. I then ask the client to be open to the possibilities, so we can create a clear picture of what they really want their business or career to do for them.

I would like to do that with you now. It won't be quite as effective as if we were coaching on the phone together, but I hope it will plant some seeds. Perhaps working on this exercise will open some possibilities for you. You may even want to work with me in one of my coaching groups or find another coach that will also be a great fit for you.

Work through the questions listed on the following pages in your journal, notebook or computer file. Keep at it. If you can't think of an answer, just ponder the question for a while but come back to it. Remember success comes from you. You need to start by knowing what it means to you before you can create it.

It is helpful to break the question "What do you want your business or career to do for you?" down into two sections: TANGIBLE which usually includes financial considerations and the INTANGIBLE which usually includes spiritual and quality of life considerations. When answering these questions, please remember that you are exploring all of the possibilities. You are not looking at how to make this happen yet. I just want you to really explore the possibilities, have fun, and dream a bit. Really discover what you want your business or career to do for you.

Once you have explored all of the possibilities, your next step may be hiring a coach to help you make them a reality. So don't hold back. Really explore what you want. Keep answering the same questions and go deeper each time. Be more specific. Be sincere. And answer the questions with your heart – not your head!

## Questions related to your financial side:

- What do you want your business or career to do for you?

- How much money do you want to make? If you replied "enough to pay your bills," how much is that?

- Do you just want to pay your bills? What else from a financial side do you want your business or career to do for you?

- Do you want a vacation? Where? How long? How often?

- Do you want to save for retirement? How long do you have to save? What kind of lifestyle will you have?

- How much money do you want to put away each month?

- How much money do you need to comfortably pay all of your current bills?

- Are you enjoying and benefiting from the things you are currently spending your money on? If yes, how? If no, what keeps you spending money on these things?

- What other area regarding finances do you want your business or career to do for you?

- Do you want to buy a house?

- Have enough money for college tutition?

- Give to charities and be more philaenthropic?

- Are you taking workshops, reading books and doing other things to support your lifelong learning?

Now let's look at the intangible side – the areas that speak more to your heart, your spirit. These are the things that fulfill you, give you a sense of satisfaction, a sense of pride and accomplishment.

### Questions related to your intangible side:

- What do you want your business or career to do for you from the intangible side? Did you answer something like, "Give me security"?

- Tell me more about this "security." What does security look like to you? How will you feel secure?

- What else do you want your business or career to do for you?

- Do you want more time?

- More freedom?

- A sense of purpose?

- A feeling of being complete?

I would like you to take some time to really explore the question of "What do I want my business or career to do for me?" Then using your journal, notebook, or computer file, describe in detail what would it look like if your business or career gave you the *soul of success.*

# Building Your Momentum

*"Dream lofty dreams, and as you dream, so shall you become.*
*Your vision is the promise of what you shall at last unveil."*
~ *John Ruskin*

Life is about being – being who you are, where you are right now, and continually moving forward. I hope you have found this book helpful and you will use the ideas and tools to move you forward to the *soul of success*. My wish for you is take the thoughts, insights, resistance, and shifts that occurred as you read the book and use them in your own unique way.

The book may change your life because you agreed with the ideas I shared or because you disagreed. It doesn't matter either way, because this experience is just one more in the vast array of experiences along your life journey. The key to life is moving forward from where you are at this very moment in the direction you truly desire.

As a coach, one of my goals is to support people to become independent. Accomplishment is about getting them to a place where they can go and not need me anymore. I have included daily and weekly practices that you can customize and make your own. You can use them to move you forward to the *soul of success*.

### Daily Practices for Achieving the Soul of Success

### MORNING RECITAL

The inner critic is one of the biggest obsticles to creating success on our own terms. The doubts, demons, and Limiting Beliefs that it brings into our mind every day can be crippling. We must counteract this never ending babble. Otherwise, it can stop us dead in our tracks from achieving what is most important to us.

Creating your own morning recital to replace the inner critic's voice will help set the right tone for the day.

### Steps to Morning Recital:

1.  Choose three phrases that you will repeat at the beginning of each day:

    *   Phrase #1 is a reflection of how much you love yourself.
    *   Phrase #2 is a reflection of having an open heart.
    *   Phrase #3 is a reflection of doing your best.

2.  Repeat each phrase aloud five times.
    *   Connect with the phrase and making it be true.
    *   Change your phrases daily or keep the same ones.

*Example:*

*I am a good person and I have a lot to offer others.*
*I will judge nothing that occurs today.*
*I will do my best in each moment, not comparing my best to any other moment.*

Throughout the day, listen for other evidence you receive that enhances the phrase and feelings from your morning recital. This exercise will give you a new script to replace the one from the inner critic. Looking for evidence throughout the day will give you tangible evidence to use against the false feelings the inner critic wants you to listen to.

## FIVE MINUTES OF GRATITUDE

We need to focus on what we want to bring into our lives. By spending five minutes every day thinking and feeling in a space of gratitude, you will keep your mind open and focused on what you want to create in your life.

This exercise can be done any time during the day – just after taking a shower, when you have finished your coffee break, after doing some yoga, etc. The key is to devote your complete awareness, attention, and emotions to standing in the space of complete gratatude.

### *Steps to Five Minutes of Gratitude:*

* Stand or sit quietly. Take three, deep cleansing breaths in through your nose and out through your mouth.

* Quiet your mind and remove all frustration and struggle.

* Put your awareness on your life and softly speak about the things you are grateful for. Say each one in a positive, clear statement.

<u>Example:</u>
*I am grateful for the comfortable clothes I am wearing.*
*I am grateful for being alive on this gloriuos day.*
*I am grateful for knowing Diane.*
*I am grateful for the delicious coffee I just had.*
*I am grateful for the opportunity to share my strengths with others.*

Build on the sense of well-being by incorporating what you are grateful for into your conversations throughout the day. Change every thought of complaint into a thought of gratitude. Move your conversation from one of struggle and discontent to one of challenge and fulfilment.

## WHAT I HAVE ACCOMPLISHED TODAY

Don't write any more daily "To Do" lists! Replace them with "What I Have Accomplished Today" list that you write at the end of each day.

There are two powerful reasons why the "What I Have Accomplished Today" list differs from "To Do" lists:

1.    You don't set yourself up to fail.
2.    You can review your daily successes and think positively about your accomplishments.

Writing this list will show you all of the things that you accomplished in the day, but usually ignore or forget because you are so busy looking at what you didn't complete.

*How to Write Your List:*

- Schedule 10 minutes daily to reflect on everything you accomplished. This time could be before you leave the office or at the end your day.

- First, you should include the TANGIBLES on your list. *Examples: Wrote two reports. Mailed off contracts. Had a great call with my coach.*

- Secondly, you should include the INTANGIBLES. *Examples: Took a walk at lunch. Did a five minute meditation. Spent time thinking about what really satisfies me at work.*

To achieve the *soul of success*, you need to balance the BEING OF SUCCESS and the DOING OF SUCCESS. The "What I Have Accomplished Today" list a practical tool to help you do just that.

## Weekly Practices for Achieving the Soul of Success

These weekly practices need to be planned out on Sunday evening or first thing Monday morning. Sunday evening is best because you can be more thoughtful and relaxed. Once you get in the habit of doing these weekly practices, you will find that they only take about 20-30 minutes. The amount of energy, time, and feeling of success you gain will make it feel like you have added hours of stress-free time to every week.

### SCHEDULE A DATE WITH YOURSELF

This week, schedule a two-hour date with yourself. This time needs to be just for you. *No work. No obligations. No combining errands or other things you need to get done.* Following are examples of what you might enjoy doing on this date:

- Go to the park
- Have a massage

- Go to a movie and have ice cream
- Go for a drive
- Read a good book
- Go to a workshop

### SOUL OF SUCCESS ACTION STEP

Write down one action step you will take this week to move you forward in achieving the *soul of success*.

- Make it specific.
- Make it measurable.
- State a time of completion for it.
- Ask for help if needed to complete it.

--------

*"Creativity is... seeing something that doesn't*
*exist already. You need to find out how you can bring it into*
*being and that way be a playmate with God."*
*~ Michele Shea*

## Book List

This list contains books recommended by friends and colleagues, as well as some of my favorites. All of these books have touched us and made a profound difference in our lives.

**Play to Win: Choosing Growth Over Fear in Work and Life**
Larry and Hersch Wilson

**Think and Grow Rich**
Napoleon Hill

**Excuse Me Your Life Is Waiting**
Lynn Grabhorn

**True Success**
Tom Morris

**Self Matters**
Phil McGraw

**The Power of Focus**
Les Hewitt

**Now Discover Your Strengths**
Marcus Buckingham, Donald O' Clifton

**Life Was Never Meant To Be A Struggle**
Stuart Wilde

**Write It Down and Make It Happen**
Henriette Anne Klauser

**Feel the Fear and Do It Anyway**
Susan Jeffers, Ph.D

**The Power of Now**
Eckhart Tolle

**Living Your Best Life**
Laura Berman Fortgang

**Inner Peace for Busy People**
Joan Borysenko

**Stand Up for Your Life**
Cheryl Richardson

**Fearless Living**
Rhonda Britten

**Man's Search for Meaning**
Victor Frankl

**Finding Your Own North Star**
Martha Beck

**Emotional Intelligence**
Daniel Goleman

**The Coaching Revolution**
David Logan, Ph.D & John King

**Under the Tuscan Sun**
Francis Mayes

**Embracing Fear**
Thom Ruttledge

**The Art of Possibility**
Benjamin and Rosamund Zander

**SmartMatch Alliances:** Achieve Extraordinary Business Growth and Success!
Judy Feld and Ernest Oriente www.coachingsuccess.com/books

**The Four Agreements**
Don Miguel Ruiz

**The International Coach Federation**
www.coachfederation.org
Directory of coaches and accredited coach training schools

**Coach U**
www.coachu.com
The premiere coach training school

**Looking for a coach?  Search the following directory:**
http://www.findacoach.com/

**Stop dreaming about a trip to Italy and make it Happen !**
www.italiantravelcoach.com

**Tap into your intuition for success in life, relationships, career.**
www.creativespirit.com

> "Look and you will find it –
> what is unsought will go undetected."
> ˜ Sophocles

# *NOTES*

## Quick Order Form

**Web orders** www.soulofsuccess.com
**Postal orders** Essence Press P.O. Box 514 West Tisbury MA 02568

Please send me # _____ of copies of the Soul of Success **$24.00** for each copy, includes shipping and handling.  Order Total: _____

**Name:** _____

**Address:** _____

**City:** _____ **Sate:** _____ **Zip:** _____

**Telephone:** _____

**Email address:** _____

Payment:
- ❏  Check
- ❏  Credit card

Card Number : _____

Name on Card: _____

Exp. Date: _____/_____

Essence Press offers discounts for volume orders. Call 1-866-902-6224 for more information.

Please send more information on:
- ❏  Coaching
- ❏  Workshops/ Seminars
- ❏  Speaking
- ❏  Teleclasses

## Quick Order Form

**Web orders** www.soulofsuccess.com
**Postal orders** Essence Press P.O. Box 514 West Tisbury MA 02568

Please send me # _____ of copies of the Soul of Success **$24.00** for each copy, includes shipping and handling.  Order Total: _____

**Name:** _____

**Address:** _____

**City:**_____ **Sate:** _____ **Zip:** _____

**Telephone:** _____

**Email address:** _____

Payment:
- ❑   Check
- ❑   Credit card

Card Number : _____

Name on Card: _____

Exp. Date: _____ / _____

Essence Press offers discounts for volume orders. Call 1-866-902-6224 for more information.

Please send more information on:
- ❑   Coaching
- ❑   Workshops/ Seminars
- ❑   Speaking
- ❑   Teleclasses

## About the Author
**BZ Riger-Hull, Essence Strategist and Executive Coach connecting limitless possibilities and measurable results.©**

Finding success on our own terms is what we're all really looking for... ways to improve our effectiveness, our happiness, and our whole quality of life. We want to live a life that is rich, meaningful, and with a sense of purpose. It must be filled with what's important to us, rather than living according to someone else's measures of success or things that seem urgent but aren't really essential.

Coach BZ Riger-Hull specializes in supporting people to find just that. Her clients say that she has the remarkable skill of spanning two worlds: the one of the practical, where we need astute business solutions and decision making skills; and the one of intuitive inner wisdom, where our personal journey of success and life gives us experience, wisdom, and insight that is pure and wise. In her coaching and training, BZ is the conduit or the point where people can relate, make a connection, and then stretch themselves and flow into tapping and trusting their own inner wisdom.

Her unique skill allows BZ to support her clients in moving through situations effectively and in the moment. They are able to transform the overwhelming and the challenging into opportunity.

BZ's rich life as an entrepreneur and businesswoman has created a strong platform to work most effectively with: Entrepreneurs, Coaches, Business Professionals, Executives, and Organizations. She specializes in:

| | |
|---|---|
| **Nuance of Communication-** | **Personal Leadership-** |
| **Connection Marketing-** | **Confidence Balance-** |

**Affiliations and Memberships-**
BZ is a certified "four agreements" Facilitator giving workshops and tele-courses on the work of don Miguel Ruiz's best selling book and teachings *The Four Agreements*. She is a graduate of Coach U, the premier international certified graduate coach training program and affiliated with the International Coach Federation.

BZ and her family live in the beautiful rolling countryside of Martha's Vineyard where she is the principal of her own successful business:
**Inspiros- Inspiration Possibilities Solutions**

BZ offers individual and group coaching over the phone and workshops, presentation, keynotes and teleclasses over the phone.

**Contact** Coach BZ at 1-866-90-COACH or email BZ@In-Spiros.com. www.In-Spiros.com

We would love your feedback on the book and what changes you have made in your life since taking action to create success on your own terms.

You can drop us a snail mail note At
Essence Press
Feedback
P.O. Box 514
West Tisbury Ma 02568
Or
Email your comments to
BZ@soulofsuccess.com